"Carl Trueman is one of the truly vital thinkers of our time. In *Strange New World*, he explains just how the West's preoccupation with a navel-gazing concern for emotional 'authenticity' has crippled our ability to think—and is consequently undermining the future of our civilization. A true must-read."

Ben Shapiro, Host, *The Ben Shapiro Show*; Editor Emeritus, The Daily Wire; author, *The Authoritarian Moment*

"At last, one of the most important books of the century is available in a more accessible format for the general reader! If you are confused about the moral and spiritual chaos overtaking Western civilization, and anguished over the seeming impotence of Christianity to stop the collapse, *Strange New World* is the book you absolutely must read. Here, in a single volume, is the best diagnosis of our cultural crisis. Anyone who wants to get themselves and their children and communities through this new dark age with their faith and sanity intact needs to read Carl Trueman's blockbuster."

Rod Dreher, author, *The Benedict Option* and *Live Not by Lies*

"As I have traveled the world, I have often hired tour guides to lead me through unfamiliar locations. Their expertise has always proven helpful in explaining what I am seeing and experiencing. And in much the same way, *Strange New World* is essentially a guided tour to modern times. Trueman acts as a wise and trusted guide to a culture that has become increasingly uncomfortable and unfamiliar. I highly recommend you take the tour."

Tim Challies, blogger, Challies.com

"An essential primer on how the world went mad. Trueman traces the origin and history of our worst ideas so that the nonscholar can understand why so many intellectuals are talking complete nonsense with such absolute conviction. A good read, a smart read, and an important read."

Andrew Klavan, author, *The Great Good Thing*; host, *The Andrew Klavan Show*

"Carl Trueman is one of the most important public intellectuals of our time, and this book, *Strange New World*, should be required reading for anyone seeking to understand our present age. Trueman offers a brilliant analysis of the modern mind, the autonomous self, identity politics, and the sexual revolution. This book demonstrates courage on every page, and the reader will draw courage from reading it. Read it and tell your friends about it."

R. Albert Mohler Jr., President and Centennial Professor of Christian Theology, The Southern Baptist Theological Seminary

"In a rare combination of erudition and clarity, Carl Trueman explains us to ourselves. From Rousseau and the Romantics, through Nietzsche, Marx, and Freud, to today's increasingly incoherent gender theorists, Trueman outlines the history of ideas that brought us almost ineluctably to this moment. But he doesn't leave us here; by revealing the wrong turns, he maps out a way forward, all the while manifesting the integrity and charity of a true gentleman. In a world of confusion, *Strange New World* is crystal clear; its author, the teacher we need today."

Erika Bachiochi, author, *The Rights of Women: Reclaiming a Lost Vision*

"This book is a You Are Here marker for disoriented pilgrims in postmodernity. Its sober analysis of where we are and how we got here will equip readers to engage contemporary confusion over identity. *Strange New World* makes the important argument of Carl Trueman's earlier work, *The Rise and Triumph of the Modern Self*, widely accessible and an excellent resource for classrooms, small groups, and individual inquiry."

Jennifer Patterson, Director of the Institute of Theology and Public Life, Reformed Theological Seminary

Strange New World

Strange New World

*How Thinkers and Activists Redefined Identity
and Sparked the Sexual Revolution*

Carl R. Trueman

Foreword by Ryan T. Anderson

CROSSWAY®

WHEATON, ILLINOIS

Cover design: Spencer Fuller, Faceout Studios

Cover image: Getty Images, Wikimedia Commons

First printing 2022

Printed in the United States of America

Trade paperback ISBN: 978-1-4335-7930-1
ePub ISBN: 978-1-4335-7933-2
PDF ISBN: 978-1-4335-7931-8
Mobipocket ISBN: 978-1-4335-7932-5

Library of Congress Cataloging-in-Publication Data

Names: Trueman, Carl R., author.
Title: Strange new world : how thinkers and activists redefined identity and sparked the sexual revolution / Carl R. Trueman ; foreword by Ryan T. Anderson.
Description: Wheaton, Illinois : Crossway, 2022. | Includes bibliographical references and index.
Identifiers: LCCN 2021028882 (print) | LCCN 2021028883 (ebook) | ISBN 9781433579301 (trade paperback) | ISBN 9781433579318 (pdf) | ISBN 9781433579325 (mobipocket) | ISBN 9781433579332 (epub)
Subjects: LCSH: Group identity—Political aspects—History. | Identity politics—History. | Sexual freedom—History.
Classification: LCC HM753 .T74 2022 (print) | LCC HM753 (ebook) | DDC 305.09—dc23
LC record available at https://lccn.loc.gov/2021028882
LC ebook record available at https://lccn.loc.gov/2021028883

Crossway is a publishing ministry of Good News Publishers.

LB		32	31	30	29	28	27	26	25	24	23
15	14	13	12	11	10	9	8	7	6	5	4	3

For David and Ann Hall

Contents

Foreword

IN LATE 2020, while the world was on lockdown due to Covid-19, Carl Trueman published one of the most important books of the past several decades. In *The Rise and Triumph of the Modern Self: Cultural Amnesia, Expressive Individualism, and the Road to Sexual Revolution*, Trueman built on insights of contemporary thinkers such as Charles Taylor, Philip Rieff, and Alasdair MacIntyre to show how modern thinkers and artists such as Jean-Jacques Rousseau, Friedrich Nietzsche, Karl Marx, Charles Darwin, Percy Bysshe Shelley, and William Blake gave expression to a worldview—what Taylor calls a "social imaginary"—that made possible and plausible the arguments of the late modern theorists who shaped the postmodern sexual revolution, people such as Sigmund Freud, Wilhelm Reich, and Herbert Marcuse. It is a penetrating analysis of several hundred years of recent intellectual history to show why people are willing to believe ideas today that every one of our grandparents would have rejected out of hand—without need of argument, evidence, or proof—just two generations ago.

The only problem? The book was over four hundred pages long. And most people have never heard of—let alone had any familiarity with—many of the names I listed above. While a pointy-headed academic like me viewed that as a feature, not a bug, in a learned tome of intellectual history, I knew that many of Carl's potential readers would not have the time or appetite to wade through so many of his finer, nuanced discussions. So I emailed Carl, praising the book as essential reading at our moment in time for scholarly specialists to digest and wrestle with, as they considered how we got here—and what we need to do to return to sanity. But I also suggested that he consider writing a shorter, more accessible version of the basic argument for nonspecialists who would benefit from the essential narrative, to better understand the historical moment in which they find themselves, and to inform the work they do in ministry, culture, politics, business, and, most importantly, raising the next generation. Carl has now produced that volume, and it sparkles on every page. In your hands is the primer every American who cares about a sound anthropology and healthy culture needs to read.

At the risk of oversimplifying what Trueman accomplishes, I would summarize the broad arc of his work as an account of how the person became a self, the self became sexualized, and sex became politicized. Of course, the person of the Psalms, of St. Paul's epistles, and of St. Augustine's *Confessions* was also a "self" in the sense of having an interior life. But the inward turn of the biblical tradition was at the service of the outward turn toward God. The "self" that Western civilization cultivated, up until just a few hundred years ago, was what Harvard political theorist Michael Sandel described as an "encumbered" self, in contrast to modernity's "unencumbered" self.[1] The person was a creature of God, who sought to conform himself to the truth, to objective moral standards, in pursuit of eternal life. Modern man, however, seeks to be "true to himself." Rather than conform thoughts, feelings, and actions to objective reality, man's inner life itself becomes the source of truth. The modern self finds himself in the midst of what Robert Bellah has described as a culture of "expressive individualism"—where each of us seeks to give expression to our individual inner lives rather than seeing ourselves as embedded in communities and bound by natural and supernatural laws.[2] Authenticity to inner feelings, rather than adherence to transcendent truths, becomes the norm.

This modern self, then, is not accountable to the theologians who preach on how to conform oneself to God but to the therapists who counsel how to be true to oneself—thus giving rise to what Philip Rieff described as the "triumph of the therapeutic."[3] And it is this therapeutic self that then becomes sexualized. Whereas for most of human history our sexual embodiment was a rather uninteresting sheer given, allowing us to unite conjugally and form families, the modern therapeutic turn inward counsels people to be true to their inner sexual desires. What was once simply self-evident, that a boy should grow up to be a man to become a husband and assume the responsibilities of a father, now entails a search to discover an inner truth about "gender identity" and "sexual orientation" based on emotions and will rather than nature and reason. Historically, one's "gender identity" was determined by one's bodily sex, as was one's "sexual orientation"—a male's "identity" was a man, and he was "oriented" by nature and reason to unite with a woman, regardless of where his (fallen) desires might incline him.

But if our sexuality is our deepest and most important inner truth, and politics is about the promotion of the truth, then it was inevitable that sex would be politicized. Whereas cultures used to cultivate the virtues that made family and religion flourish, now the law would be used to suppress these institutions as they stood in the way of sexual "authenticity," as politics sought to create a world where it was safe—and free from criticism—to follow one's sexual desires. Hence, the push to redefine marriage legally was never really about joint tax returns and hospital visitation but about forcing churches to update their doctrines and bakers to affirm same-sex relationships. Affirmation of the sexualized self is the key to our new politics. And our new language. Even what was once called sex "reassignment" surgery is now known as gender "affirmation" procedures. And federal mandates will punish you if you object.

None of this is to suggest that ideas alone explain our current cultural moment. After all, if there were not plastic surgery to create entities that resemble genitalia, and synthetic testosterone and estrogen to "masculinize" and "feminize" bodies, few would seriously entertain the idea that sex could be "reassigned"—since it was not "assigned" to begin with. How we deploy various technological advances, and how we even think about the concept of technology, are deeply influenced by ideas, either explicitly in the case of intellectuals or implicitly via the social imaginary. The idea that the will should master nature—creation—is, after all, plausible only under certain conditions.

Any effective response, then, would need to challenge those long-brewing conditions, both intellectually and culturally. Trueman calls the church to preach sound doctrine boldly, to live in an intentional and countercultural way according to biblical and liturgical seasons—to embody and promote an alternative social imaginary—and challenge the sexual revolution both from above and from below. From above by exposing the various misguided preconditions that make the sexual revolution plausible, and from below by demonstrating the truth about the human person and the body—so that there is no tension between faith and reason, science and revelation. Most importantly, Trueman calls on the church not only to bear witness to the truth but to be a place of belonging for the broken, forming community and living culturally. Families, in particular, will need to consider what this means in the formation of their children. Simply attending church each Sunday will not cut it anymore (if it ever did). Socially embodied ways of living in conformity with ultimate realities will prove essential.

In 2018, I published a book titled *When Harry Became Sally: Responding to the Transgender Moment*. The title was meant to suggest two things: that transgender ideology was not the truth about man but was the result of various cultural forces producing this "moment" in history, and that within one generation, popular culture had gone from questioning whether a man and a woman could be "just friends" in *When Harry Met Sally* to declaring there was a civil right for a man to become a woman. In *Strange New World*, Trueman uncovers and describes the deep underlying social and intellectual forces that explain why his grandfather would have rejected such a claim without second thought while President Biden declares, "Transgender equality is the civil rights issue of our time."[4]

I have long admired Carl's popular essays and academic books. This book is the best of both worlds, combining his accessible writing and deep learning. I am deeply grateful that this book is his first major publication as a Fellow at the Ethics and Public Policy Center, and honored that he asked me to write this foreword. May it bear abundant fruit.

Ryan T. Anderson
President, Ethics and Public Policy Center

Preface

THIS SHORT BOOK is not a precise précis of my larger work, *The Rise and Triumph of the Modern Self*, but covers the same ground in a briefer and (hopefully) more accessible format. Readers who want the full argument, along with the detailed footnotes, should consult the longer work.

As always, I have incurred numerous debts along the way. Ryan Anderson first encouraged me to think about putting the argument of the larger book into a concise form so that it might be more useful to hard-pressed Washington staffers. He also generously provided the foreword. As always, Justin Taylor and the staff at Crossway were incredibly supportive of the project. Special thanks is also due to the following: Paul Helm for reading and commenting on drafts of chapters 5 and 6 in light of helpful criticism he made of the earlier book; the Institute for Faith and Freedom at Grove City College for generously funding not one but two research assistants during the academic year, 2020–21; Emma Peel and Joy Zavalick, the two aforementioned assistants, whose infectious enthusiasm, diligent editing, and work on the study questions and glossary— the latter of which I encourage you to consult if you encounter an unfamiliar term—greatly improved the final product; and, as always, my wife, Catriona, whose support of my work these many years has proved essential.

The book is dedicated to David and Ann Hall for their faithful ministry and dear friendship.

Welcome to This Strange New World

Introduction

Many of us are familiar with books and movies whose plots revolve around central characters finding themselves trapped in a world where nothing behaves in quite the way they expect. Perhaps Lewis Carroll's *Alice in Wonderland* and *Alice Through the Looking-Glass* might be the classic examples of this in children's literature. But this is a standard plotline in many other works. From Franz Kafka's *The Trial* to *The Matrix* series of movies, dystopian confusion is a hardy perennial of our culture.

Yet this phenomenon is no longer confined to the fictional products of our day. For many people, the Western world in which we now live has a profoundly confusing, and often disturbing, quality to it. Things once regarded as obvious and unassailable virtues have in recent years been subject to vigorous criticism and even in some cases come to be seen by many as more akin to vices. Indeed, it can seem as if things that almost everybody believed as unquestioned orthodoxy the day before yesterday—that marriage is to be between one man and one woman, for example—are now regarded as heresies advocated only by the dangerous, lunatic fringe.

Nor are the problems confined to the world "out there." Often, they manifest themselves most acutely and most painfully within families. Parents teaching their family traditional views of sex find themselves met with incomprehension by their children who have absorbed far different views from the culture around them. What a parent considers to be a loving response to a child struggling with same-sex attraction or gender dysphoria might be regarded by the child as hateful and bigoted. And this is as true within the church as it is within wider society. The generation gap today is reflected not simply in fashion and music but in attitudes and beliefs about some of the most basic aspects of human existence. The result is often confusion and sometimes even heartbreak as many of the most brutal engagements in the culture war are played out around the dinner table and at family gatherings.

Welcome to this strange new world. You may not like it. But it is where you live, and therefore it is important that you try to understand it.

Of course, all this cultural flux and instability is profoundly dis-orienting, especially for those of the older generation but even for those who are younger, as the gulf between what their peers think and what their parents believe can now seem vaster than ever. And even the more self-aware of the older generation can often be left wondering whether opinions they have held since childhood are really true or whether they are simply the result of their upbring-ing. Did not generations of otherwise normal people believe that slavery was acceptable? Did society not once consider the death penalty for even comparatively trivial criminal offences to be ap-propriate and just? Does this not mean that traditional views on sex, marriage, and gender might also have been seriously misplaced or perhaps have outlived their usefulness in our modern, globalized, technological society? Such questions are appropriate, given the errors of the past with regard to significant moral questions.

The challenge, of course, is how to begin to engage in this type of reflection. Part of the confusion is caused by the fact that so many areas of our lives and world seem to be in flux that there seems very little that is solid or constant by which we can navigate the apparent chaos around us. Yet it is my conviction that there is something that helps to unify the changes we are witnessing and to make them, if not entirely explicable, at least less random than we might be tempted to think. This is the notion of the *self*. And the self connects to three other concepts of relevance to my narrative: expressive individualism, the sexual revolution, and the social imaginary. So, before we begin the story proper, it is important to define exactly how I shall be using these terms.

What Is the *Self*?

The term *self* needs some explanation. There is a commonsensical way in which we use the idea of being a self to refer to our basic consciousness of ourselves as individual people. I know that I am Carl Trueman, an Englishman living in America, not Jeff Bezos, who founded Amazon, or Donald Trump, who was president of the United States. Those two are different individuals, different selves because they are different self-conscious beings with different bodies, minds, and life-stories from me.

When I use the term *self* in this book, I am referring not to this commonsense way of using the term but rather to the deeper notion of where the "real me" is to be found, how that shapes my view of life, and in what the fulfillment or happiness of that "real me" consists. Perhaps this is best expressed by a series of questions. Am I, for example, to be understood primarily in terms of my obligations toward, and dependence upon, others? Does education consist in training me in the demands and expectations of the wider culture and forming me, shaping me into that which will serve the community at large? Is "growing up" a process by which I learn to control my feelings, to act with restraint, and sacrifice my desires to those of the community around me? Or am I to understand myself as born free and able to create my own identity? Does education consist in enabling me to express outwardly that which I feel inwardly? Is growing up a process not of learning restraint but rather of capitalizing on opportunities to perform? My conviction is that the normative self of today—the typical way in which we each think of our identity—is one who answers those last three questions in the affirmative. The modern self assumes the authority of inner feelings and sees authenticity as defined by the ability to give social expression to the same. The modern self also assumes that society at large will recognize and affirm this behavior. Such a self is defined by what is called expressive individualism.

What Is Expressive Individualism?

The term "expressive individualism" was coined by the American scholar Robert Bellah, who defines it as follows:

> Expressive individualism holds that each person has a unique core of feeling and intuition that should unfold or be expressed if individuality is to be realized.[1]

Canadian philosopher Charles Taylor, too, sees this expressive individualism as the normative modern notion of selfhood in the

West. He specifically connects it to what he dubs "the culture of 'authenticity,'" which he describes as follows:

> [The culture of authenticity is one where] each one of us has his/her own way of realizing our humanity, and that it is important to find and live out one's own, as against surrendering to conformity with a model imposed on us from outside, by society, or the previous generation, or religious or political authority.[2]

In short, the modern self is one where authenticity is achieved by acting outwardly in accordance with one's inward feelings. As we shall see in subsequent chapters, this notion is now very deep in modern culture and helps to explain a host of interesting phenomena. For example, the increasing social sensitivity to criticizing anyone for their personal lifestyle choice reflects a view of the world where each person is free to perform life in whatever way they choose; and any attempt to express disapproval is therefore a blow not simply against particular ways of behaving but against the right of that person to be whoever they wish to be. Indeed, we might even say that the very notion of "personal lifestyle choice" is a symptom of a society where expressive individualism is the normative way of thinking about self and its place in the world.

It is worth noting at this point that I am not here arguing that expressive individualism is an unmitigated bad thing. Human beings do have an inner life. We do feel things. We are emotional creatures. Those who are not to some degree demonstrative and emotional so often strike us as somehow less than human or as cold and indifferent. In this book, I do not wish to deny that expressive individualism has aspects that are good and commendable. I am concerned, however, with how its triumph as the normative self has led to some of the strangest and, to many, most disturbing aspects of our modern world.

Many of us are indeed particularly disturbed by the radical changes in society's sexual norms over recent decades, and even more so by the rise of the transgender movement. It is my belief, however, that these elements of what we call the sexual revolution are actually symptoms of this wider turn to expressive individualism in the West. The priority that the LGBTQ+ movement places on sexual desire and inner feelings relative to personal identity is part of this broader accent on the inner, psychological life of Western people that shapes us all. It is my contention in this book that expressive individualism provides the broad backdrop to these aspects of what is commonly called the sexual revolution.

What Is the Sexual Revolution?

When we hear the term *sexual revolution*, many of us are tempted to think of the ways in which sexual morality has been transformed since the 1960s. Often, we tend to assume that these changes involve the expansion of the range of socially acceptable sexual behavior. That certainly captures something of what I mean by the term. For example, we now live in an age where homosexuality no longer carries the social stigma, let alone the criminal penalties, that it once did. Further, sex outside of marriage—indeed, outside of any framework of personal commitment—is now commonplace. Our sexual world is simply not that of our Victorian ancestors.

Yet it would be a mistake to see the sexual revolution merely in terms of a loosening of moral boundaries to include more forms of sexual expression. What marks the modern sexual revolution out as distinctive is the way it has normalized sexual phenomena such as homosexuality and promiscuity and even come to celebrate them. It is not therefore the fact that, for example, modern people engage in gay sex or look at sexually explicit material, while earlier generations did not, that constitutes the sexual revolution. It is that gay sex and the use of pornography no longer involve the shame and social stigma they once did. Indeed, they have even come to be regarded as a normal part of mainstream culture.

In short, the sexual revolution does not simply represent a growth in the routine transgression of traditional sexual codes or even a modest expansion of the boundaries of what is and is not acceptable sexual behavior. Not at all. Rather, it is the repudiation of the very idea of such codes in their entirety. More than that, it has come in certain areas, such as that of homosexuality and transgenderism, to require the positive repudiation of traditional sexual mores to the point where belief in, or maintenance of, such views has come to be seen as ridiculous and even a sign of serious mental or moral deficiency. And to understand this, we need to see the sexual revolution as a particularly sharp manifestation of the characteristics of expressive individualism. If the individual's inner identity is defined by sexual desire, then he or she must be allowed to act out on that desire in order to be an authentic person.

Obviously, Western society still has sexual codes and places limits on sexual behavior—pedophilia, for example, continues to be outlawed in the United States—but those limits are increasingly defined not so much by the sex acts themselves as by the issue of whether the parties involved have consented to those acts. Again, notice what the sexual revolution has done: it has brought us to the point where sexual acts in themselves are seen as having no intrinsic moral significance; it is the consent (or not) of those engaging in them that provides the moral framework.

Why Do We Think the Way We Do?

At the heart of this book is a historical narrative that is concerned primarily with the ideas of a number of intellectual figures, from Jean-Jacques Rousseau and Mary Wollstonecraft through to Germaine Greer and Yuval Levin. And yet if my thesis is correct—that expressive individualism is the default setting for understanding our selves in the twenty-first century—the obvious question to ask is: How did this come about, when so few people today have heard of, let alone read, the various thinkers that I discuss?

The answer is that these thinkers do not "cause" the rise of the modern self or the sexual revolution in any simple or direct way, as a ball hitting a window might cause the glass to shatter. Many other factors come into play, as I shall note particularly in chapters 5 and 6. I did choose these thinkers partly because they have proved influential in elite circles. Rousseau, for example, has had a profound effect on modern educational theory, and Nietzsche, via the work of people such as Michel Foucault, on the study of the humanities. But I also chose them because they offer, in particularly clear and helpful ways, examples of people who reflected self-consciously on the kind of shifts in our ways of thinking, such that they allow us to understand more clearly the implications of certain assumptions and intuitions that we may unreflectively have absorbed from the world around us. But in no sense is the intellectual story I trace here a fully sufficient causal account of how the modern self came to be. As I noted, few if any of us have read their works.

So if people are not reading Rousseau and company, why do so many of their ideas shape the way we think about the world? The answer is that their thinking captures important aspects of what Charles Taylor calls "the social imaginary." It is an awkward term, using an adjective, *imaginary*, as if it were a noun. But as it is established in the literature, and as it does convey an important concept, it is nonetheless useful for my project.

Taylor defines the social imaginary as follows:

> I speak of "imaginary" (i) because I'm talking about the way ordinary people "imagine" their social surroundings, and this is often not expressed in theoretical terms, it is carried in images, stories, legends, etc. But it is also the case that (ii) theory is often the possession of a small minority, whereas what is interesting in the social imaginary is that it is shared by large groups of people, if not the whole society. Which leads to a third difference: (iii) the social imaginary is that common understanding which makes possible common practices, and a widely shared sense of legitimacy.[3]

What Taylor is pointing to here is the fact that human beings do not typically think about themselves and the world they inhabit in consistently self-conscious terms. Rather, we *imagine* it to be in certain ways—physically and indeed morally.

Thus, for example, when I rise from my desk and go to the kitchen for a cup of tea during a break from writing, I do not spend time reflecting on the physics of solids and gases. Indeed, I have only a very minimal understanding of such. But I do leave my study via the hole called the doorway, and not through the walls. That is an intuitive action. Similarly, in the realm of morals, much of my response to the world around me is instinctive. If I see a person being mugged, I move to help them myself or by calling for assistance. I do not need to reflect upon Aristotelian or

Kantian arguments about ethics. I simply react instinctively because I intuitively know both that the situation is wrong and what I need to do in response.

So when Taylor directs us to the social imaginary, he is making the point that the way we think about the world is not primarily by way of rational arguments based on first principles. It is much more intuitive than that. And that means that the story of the modern self is not simply the story of big ideas thought by profound thinkers. It is the story of how the way we intuit or imagine the world has come to be. And that involves far more than books and arguments.

Think about the sexual revolution. This is more than the result of a group of radical students in the 1960s discovering the work of Wilhelm Reich. The reason society thinks about sex the way it does is the result of the confluence of a host of factors. The pill made it cheap and easy to separate sex from procreation. In short, it made sex as recreation a far more practical option than it had been before. The advent of *Playboy* and then *Cosmopolitan* in mainstream culture presented promiscuity as a cool, attractive lifestyle for men and women alike. The rise of no-fault divorce reduced marriage to a sentimental bond. The rhetoric of feminism asserted women's control over their own bodies and sexuality. The internet massively expanded the accessibility of pornography, and, as more people used it, the social stigma it traditionally carried was diminished. Soap operas and sitcoms, even commercials, presented sex as a cost-free pastime. The list goes on, but the picture is clear: a complex set of factors, from philosophy to technology to pop culture, shape the way we intuitively think about sex. Indeed, they shape the way we think about the world in general and our place within it. And that is why thinking about our situation in terms of the social imaginary is so helpful. In short, it deals with us as we are and not simply as beings constituted by a set of disembodied ideas. We do not so much think about the world as we intuitively relate to it.

Conclusion

To anticipate my argument, it is my conviction that the dramatic changes and flux we witness and experience in society today are related to the rise to cultural normativity of the expressive individual self, particularly as expressed through the idioms of the sexual revolution. And the fact that the reasons for this are so deeply embedded in all aspects of our culture means that we all are, to some extent, complicit in what we see happening around us. To put it bluntly, we all share more or less the same social imaginary.

Of course, the importance of the social imaginary points us to the fact that, if our world has no simple, single cause, our problems therefore have no simple, single solution. The modern self is the fruit of a complicated confluence of cultural factors. That can be depressing for those who hope that electing the right politician or appointing the appropriate Supreme Court justice will solve all the world's ills. But it also means that we can begin to think more constructively about how to address the issues we face. And that is the hope I have in writing this book. I offer no easy answers, but I do hope it provides a framework by which the reader is better able to understand, or be more self-conscious of, the modern Western social imaginary that shapes us all. This is neither a lament nor a polemic. Both have their place, I am sure, but here my purpose is more descriptive and explanatory. To respond to our times we must first understand our times. That is my goal.

And with that having been said, let the story of the modern self begin.

Study Questions

1. How have your beliefs and opinions been shaped by the world around you?

2. What differences in attitudes and beliefs have you noticed between the generations in your family? How have you addressed these?

3. What is expressive individualism? Do you recognize it in yourself? In what ways?

2

Romantic Roots

Introduction

If we take the most dramatic developments of the sexual revolution—say, the legitimation of transgenderism—it is interesting to ask what things wider society already needed to regard as normal in order for this to be first plausible and then normalized. The sentence "I am a woman trapped in a man's body" would have been nonsense to my grandfather. Had it been uttered by a patient to a doctor in the mid-twentieth century, the doctor would almost certainly have responded that the patient had a psychiatric problem and that his mind needed to be treated so as to bring its feelings into line with his physical body. Today, the doctor is more likely to respond that the problem is such that the patient's body needs to be brought into alignment with those inner feelings. Indeed, were a doctor to respond in the earlier fashion today, he might well find himself subject to legal action. What has changed in our society and in the social imaginary to bring this new situation about?

This question can be adequately answered only when a range of phenomena, from ideas to technology, are considered. In this chapter, however, I want to focus on one particular element in this story: the granting of decisive authority to inner feelings. A moment's reflection indicates that the doctor in the mid-twentieth century who saw what we now call gender dysphoria as a problem with the mind was working within a social imaginary that granted normative authority to the physical body. The body was decisive for answering the question of whether a person was a man or a woman, the few cases of biologically intersex people notwithstanding. Doctors today, however, grant normative authority in such cases to inner feelings or psychological convictions. We should note that this is not a "scientific" move. It is not the result of "following the science." Science can study the body and the mind and can describe and analyze how the two connect; but how the relationship between the two is constructed in terms of which has normative authority rests upon evaluative judgments shaped by wider philosophical or cultural commitments. The question for us therefore is: Where do those commitments originate?

The story of the granting of such authority to inner feelings or psychological states is a long and complex one. Of course, human beings have always been aware that they have an inner realm of reflection. The Psalms are full of introspection and emotion. The great tragedies of ancient Greece offer fascinating glimpses into human feelings such as love, anger, hatred, and revenge. Paul's New Testament letters offer glimpses into the inner conflict of the human heart. And Augustine's *Confessions* present the great bishop's autobiography as a prayer informed by extended reflection on his inner life. Yet simply acknowledging this inner dimension of human selfhood is not the same as authorizing it to have a decisive role in identity. The Psalms and Paul look inward but then understand that inward life in terms of the prior authority of the external world as ordered by God. The Greek tragedies are tragic in large part because of the moral dilemmas and challenges of the external moral order in which the protagonists are caught up. Augustine moves inward so that he can then move outward to God and to the reality that is prior to and greater than his own feelings and in light of which those feelings are to be understood. The transgender person, by contrast, sees inward, psychological conviction as the nonnegotiable reality to which all external realities must be made to conform. How did the perennial inner life of human beings come to hold such power over our identities?

René Descartes

One obvious source for this authorization of feelings, of the inner psychological space of human beings, is the French philosopher René Descartes (1596–1650). Descartes made significant contributions to the field of mathematics, but his significance to this narrative lies in his philosophy. In the wake of the fragmentation of the institutional church at the Reformation, he sought to find a basis for certain knowledge. In his *Discourse on the Method and Principles of Philosophy*, he set himself the task of doubting everything. He realized, however, that this path of radical skepticism still required the existence of a doubting subject. In doubting one's own existence, for example, one actually had to concede one's own existence as the doubting subject. This conclusion is often summarized in the phrase "I think; therefore, I am." What is of interest to my narrative is the way this places human thought—a psychological phenomenon—at the very center of the project. Thinking is the ground of certainty. This is reinforced by Descartes's dualism, articulated in his *Meditations on First Philosophy*, that posited a distinction between the mind and the body. We might say, from the vantage point of current developments, that Descartes formulated the notions of mind and body in a way that gave fundamental importance to the former and potentially set the two in opposition. Though it was not Descartes's intention so to do, establishing this psychological foundation for certainty set in place a conceptual framework that makes transgenderism plausible.

Jean-Jacques Rousseau

Of more significance, given his much broader impact on culture, is the Genevan philosopher Jean-Jacques Rousseau (1712–1778). Rousseau was a strange but brilliant man. Self-taught and multi-talented, he wrote novels and plays, tried his hand at musical composition, worked as a civil servant, and developed philosophies of society and education that continue to influence modern discussions of these topics. His thought was also an inspiration for both the French Revolution and the artistic movement now known as Romanticism. He was also a rather obstinate, nasty, and at times paranoid man. He famously fell out with the contemporary Scottish philosopher David Hume and notoriously sent all five of his children to an orphanage (and thus to almost certain early death) shortly after each was born.

Rousseau is particularly significant to our story because he offers a compelling and influential articulation of two ideas that help us understand the modern notion of the self. First, he locates identity in the inner psychological life of the individual. Feelings for Rousseau are central to who we are. And second, he sees society (or perhaps better, *culture*) as exerting a corrupting influence on the self. To the extent that society prevents us from acting consistently with our feelings, to that extent it prevents us from being who we really are. In short, society makes us inauthentic.

Identity and the Inner Life

In his autobiography, *Confessions*, Rousseau sets forth his purpose in writing as follows:

> I am resolved on an undertaking that has no model and will have no imitator. I want to show my fellow-men a man in all the truth of nature; and this man is to be myself. . . . The particular object of my confessions is to make known my inner self, exactly as it was in every circumstance of my life. It is the history of my soul that I promised, and to relate it faithfully I require no other memorandum; all I need do, as I have done up until now, is to look inside myself.[1]

To us, this is likely to sound unexceptional, even somewhat passé. We are raised on a diet of cultural products, from confessional-style talk shows through to classics of modern literature such as *To the Lighthouse*, that focus on inner feelings and our psychological lives. But in Rousseau's day, it was radical and explosive. Indeed, that we consider this to be such a nondescript statement is itself a testimony to the incredible success of this idea in shaping the social imaginary. What Rousseau proposed as something novel and exciting is now the norm. To know who a person is—in fact, to know oneself—one needs only to have access to their inner thoughts, for it is there that the real person is to be found.

With this as his guiding principle, Rousseau offers the world what is in a sense the first modern autobiography. As Rousseau recounts events from his life—an early act of theft, a lie that led to the dismissal of a maid at a house where he was employed, his loves, his career in the civil service, the events that shaped his philosophy—his focus is on his feelings, his motivations, and his emotional responses. Of course, autobiography is a self-serving genre. The reader has no guarantee that the psychological narrative is true, and certain events that would shed him in a bad light, such as the abandonment of his children, are dealt with in a remarkably cursory, unemotional manner so as to lessen their significance. But the truth of the narrative is not the important thing. It is the psychological focus of the narrative, the prioritizing of the inner life, that emerges as a paradigm for later narratives—autobiographical, biographical, and fictional.

This inward move helps to explain some of the characteristics of modern society. Take, for example, the notion of authenticity. This is the idea that the genuine person is the one who acts outwardly in a manner consistent with how they think or feel inside. In a sense, we all can agree this is a good thing. We have pejorative terms for those whose outward behavior stands at odds with what they are really thinking: hypocritical, duplicitous, two-faced. But modern society has exalted this notion of authenticity to the point where at times it cuts directly against the value that previous generations placed on restraint and self-control. In the early 1970s, for example, Richard Nixon's presidency was fatally damaged by the existence on the transcription of the Watergate tapes of the phrase "expletive deleted." The thought that the president might use foul language in discussions in the privacy of his office was deeply shocking to the American people. Today, there is barely a politician in Washington that one can name who has not at some point used profanity as part of a public speech or statement. This is symptomatic of a change in society's attitudes. Now we want our politicians to use such language because it indicates that what we hear in public is consistent with what we know they say in private. It makes us feel they are being honest with us. They are authentic.

Yet the reality is, of course, more complicated than that. While we might in principle think that it is a good thing for everyone to be "authentic" in this sense, we are also aware of limits to this notion. For example, the person who experiences a powerful inner urge to harm or even kill another person would not be regarded as hypocritical if he were to resist such. Rather, failure to do so, failure to restrain those instincts, would render him subject to accusations of being a psychopath or deeply wicked. In this instance, our language again indicates our moral evaluation of such a person. So, self-restraint even today has its place, but it is considerably more restricted as a virtue than it was.

In the story of the modern self, then, Rousseau's focus on the inner psychological life of the individual as taking us to the heart of who he or she is represents a key development in Western culture, the significance of which still has a profound effect on how we think of our identities today. And inevitably, as societies are made up of individuals, Rousseau's focus on the inner life stands in positive relation to his view of the impact of our various social arrangements on the individual. Indeed, he views these two things as mutually reinforcing. To demonstrate this, he offers an account of an event from his youth.

Society and the Individual

Early in his *Confessions*, Rousseau tells the story of how he was led to his first act of theft. A man called Verrat, who lived in the same town, persuaded Rousseau to steal asparagus from his (Verrat's) mother, to sell for money that Rousseau could then give to

Verrat to buy food. Consistent with his psychological concern, Rousseau is not particularly interested in the act of theft itself. Stealing asparagus hardly ranks as a high crime or misdemeanor. What fascinates him is the inner thought process that led him to commit this crime, and in this context he notes two things. First, the desire to help Verrat avoid going hungry was a good motive for his action. Rousseau was not driven by greed or a desire for personal gain. His sin was thus not the result of him being an intrinsically bad person. On the contrary, it speaks to an extent of his sympathy for another in need. Second, he mentions that he was also lured into committing the crime by Verrat flattering him as a talented young man. It was the fact that he liked to be liked, not that he liked doing evil, that proved his undoing.

Taken together, these two observations provide an anecdotal example of what Rousseau expresses in more theoretical terms in his famous *First and Second Discourses*: that it is society that corrupts the individual; that individual corruption is not, as, say, the Christian theologian Augustine argued, the result of an innate tendency to law-breaking inherited from our primeval ancestor, Adam. No, Rousseau rejects the Christian doctrine of original sin. We human beings are born essentially moral; it is the pressures brought to bear on us by society to conform ourselves to its conventions and demands, and our weakness toward flattery, that explain our corruption. At least in the first instance, sin is really society's fault, not ours.

Here is how Rousseau expresses it in his famous *First Discourse*, an essay he submitted to a competition where he had to answer the question "Has the progress of the sciences and the arts led to the corruption or purification of morals?" There is little doubt that the competition organizers expected an answer that affirmed the beneficial impact of the sciences and the arts. Ever the contrarian,

Rousseau gave the opposite answer. And he won first prize. Here is how he summarizes his position:

> How sweet it would be to live among us if the outward countenance were always the image of the heart's dispositions; if decency were virtue; if our maxims were our rules: if genuine Philosophy were inseparable from the title of Philosopher! . . . Before Art had fashioned our manners and taught our passions to speak in ready-made terms, our morals were rustic but natural; and differences in conduct conveyed differences of character at first glance. . . .
>
> Today, when subtler inquiries and a more refined taste have reduced the Art of pleasing to principles, a vile and deceiving uniformity prevails in our morals and all minds seem to have been cast in the same mold: constantly politeness demands, propriety commands: constantly one follows custom, never one's own genius. One no longer dares to appear what one is; and under this perpetual constraint, the men who make up the herd that is called society will, when placed in similar circumstances, all act in similar ways unless more powerful motives incline them differently.[2]

In this idea, that society is the problem and not the natural individual, we see the seed of numerous modern tendencies. For example, there is the way in which criminal justice often tilts toward taking environmental factors into consideration when adjudicating the personal responsibility of an individual for a particular crime. The idea that an abusive childhood might mitigate such responsibility is commonplace in our culture. And, of course, this notion is not entirely misplaced. Indeed, Rousseau is not wrong in his claim that environment, or culture, shapes our nature. Our backgrounds do help to form our understanding of what is and is not acceptable behavior, what our moral priorities should be, whether we respect other people's persons and property. Where Rousseau is wrong, however, is in seeing the hypothetical pristine nature of human beings as something that is instinctively empathetic and moral. As we shall see, later thinkers, most notably Friedrich Nietzsche and Sigmund Freud, will offer very different, and much darker, accounts of the inner voice of nature in which Rousseau places so much confidence. Environment and culture may shape us, but they do so within boundaries established by the basic moral tendencies of a human nature that tilts toward the dark side.

We also see here the underlying idea behind so much of modern child-centered education. If society is the problem because it perverts and corrupts the individual, then society's institutions are the tool by which this is accomplished. If we believe this, then that means that we need to revise our understanding of the function of institutions in such a way that they serve the natural individual. In short, they become places of performance, of learning to follow and then to give expression to that inner voice of nature, not places where that inner nature is to be tamed and formed into something else. The end result is much akin to that which the contemporary political scientist Yuval Levin has identified as a reversal in the nature of institutions, from places of formation to places of performance.

In fact, Rousseau's focus in *Confessions* on his inner psychology and the idea of the true self that he articulates in the *Discourses* together represent what we noted in chapter 1 is now known as *expressive individualism*, the notion that I am most truly myself when I am able to express outwardly what that voice of nature says to me inwardly. Doing that, to use modern parlance, is what makes me authentic. I noted above that this is now what we look for in our politicians—not public reserve and discipline with regard to the traditional conventions of public decorum. Letting it all hang out, to use a colloquial phrase, is what we want to do ourselves and what we expect from others.

We should also note one other implication of this: If the original, pristine individual is the truly authentic me, then not just institutions but every other person stands in a naturally adversarial relationship to me. Everyone else is first and foremost a potential threat to my authenticity.

Again, Rousseau expresses this rather neatly in his work *The Social Contract*:

Man is born free, yet everywhere he is in chains.[3]

This is, of course, complete nonsense. Of all creatures on the face of the earth, human beings are born remarkably dependent on others, and that for a remarkably long period of time. Specifically, we are utterly dependent upon our parents from birth for some years. No newborn child, left alone and to its own devices, will survive more than a few days at most. One might therefore respond to Rousseau by saying, "Man is born utterly dependent on others but everywhere tries to persuade himself that such an obvious fact is not actually true."

Of course, that a sentence is utterly fallacious has never prevented it from being believed by large numbers of people and, on occasion, used as a foundational principle for a comprehensive philosophy of life. Such is the case with Rousseau here, and with the modern notion of the autonomous expressive individual that flows from his thought. For Rousseau, we are most ourselves when we act outwardly in accordance with that inner, pristine voice of nature because we are naturally free, independent individuals. And this ideal, free human is what later writers dubbed Rousseau's noble savage: the individual in the pristine state of nature, uncorrupted by the demands of civilized society with its hypocrisies and sharp antitheses between outward behavior and that inner voice of nature, is answerable to no one and free to be himself. That is the modern myth of selfhood that now dominates the Western imagination and that underlies the sexual revolution.

Romanticism

Rousseau's confidence in the voice of nature and distrust of the confected conventions of polite, urban society resonated with the representatives of the artistic movement that later scholars dubbed Romanticism. As with all -*isms*, a precise one-size-fits-all definition is impossible. It was not a specific club with a formal membership list but more of a cultural ethos, and one that found exemplars across Europe, especially in Germany and Great Britain. Friedrich Schiller, Friedrich Hölderlin, William Wordsworth, Samuel Taylor Coleridge, Percy Bysshe Shelley, and Lord Byron were all representatives of its literary expression. J. M. W. Turner and Caspar David Friedrich were two painters whose work reflected the Romantic impulse on canvas, as Franz Schubert and Franz Liszt were two who did so in musical composition.

At its heart, Romanticism sought to find authentic humanity in an acknowledgement of, and connection to, the power of nature. Two great examples are the poems "Mont Blanc" by Percy Bysshe Shelley and "Daffodils" by William Wordsworth. They also illustrate an extremely important point: the focus on nature that we find in the Romantics was not simply driven by a desire for a sentimental thrill found contemplating, as in these examples, the sublime vastness of a great mountain or the delicate beauty of a flower. Romanticism saw this contemplation of nature as having a deep ethical impact upon individuals who engaged in such. Meditating upon the natural wonders of the world served to reshape them morally, to reconnect them with nature and with their own true humanity and that of others. The beautiful in nature inspired delight, the sublime inspired fear and awe. And the experience of the two helped to form appropriate sentiments that shaped the moral intuitions or instincts of the individual. We might say, in modern parlance, they made the individual an emotionally healthy, empathetic person.

This idea is expressed rather beautifully in a letter written by Mary Wollstonecraft, wife of the English radical thinker William Godwin and mother of Mary Shelley, wife of Percy and author of *Frankenstein*. Wollstonecraft, one of the most remarkable intellects of the eighteenth century, speaks of nature as follows:

> Nature is the nurse of sentiment,—the true source of taste;—yet what misery, as well as rapture, is produced by a quick perception of the beautiful and sublime, when it is exercised in observing animated nature, when every beauteous feeling and emotion excites responsive sympathy, and the harmonized soul sinks into melancholy, or rises to extasy, just as the chords are touched, like the aeolian harp agitated by the changing wind. But how dangerous is it to foster these sentiments in such an imperfect state of existence; and how difficult to eradicate them when an affection for mankind, a passion for an individual, is but the unfolding of that love which embraces all that is great and beautiful.[4]

Wollstonecraft here presents the human reception of the beautiful and the sublime in nature as deeply shaping the human person, fostering love and sympathy for other individuals and indeed for all humankind. This is no dilettantish interest in the aesthetics of the natural world; it is part of a deep philosophy of nature in general and of human nature in particular. As nature has an impact upon the emotions, so it forms the person's moral sentiments or instincts in the right way.

Wollstonecraft's use of the image of the Aeolian harp is important. This was to become something commonplace in Romantic literature, used perhaps most famously by Coleridge in his poem "The Eolian Harp." Rather like the wind chimes that are so popular today, the Aeolian harp made music when the wind blew over it and caused the strings to sound. It is the perfect image for the idea that human beings are but instruments that play as they should when moved by the power of nature. As Coleridge expresses it,

> And what if all of animated nature
> Be but organic Harps diversely framed,
> That tremble into thought, as o'er them sweeps
> Plastic and vast, one intellectual breeze,
> At once the Soul of each, and God of all?[5]

Again, here we see the power of nature (and the passivity of human beings) in truly shaping what it means to be human, and this expressed in deeply religious language. Nature is powerful. And being sensitive to the voice of nature is necessary if one is to be a truly authentic human being.

The same idea is expressed in a more programmatic form in Wordsworth and Coleridge's preface to their influential collection of verse, *Lyrical Ballads*, a set of poems that generally—though not exclusively—focused on rural life and scenes from nature. The reason for this focus was simple, and one with which Rousseau would have resonated: rural life, exempt from the social ambition, rivalries, confected manners, and posturing that elite life in the city demanded, showed human beings in a more unvarnished, and thus more authentic, form. One of the poems had a title that even by the standards of the day was what we would now call "politically incorrect": "The Idiot Boy." In this poem, Wordsworth told the story of a simpleton who is sent by his mother to fetch the doctor from a nearby town to help a sick neighbor. When he does not return after several hours, his mother sets out to find him. It transpires that he never reached the doctor's house, and she finds him sitting on her pony in the forest. He had spent the night there looking at the moon and listening to the owls, mistaking them for the dawn time sun and for cockerels respectively.

A friend of Wordsworth, John Wilson, was so offended by Wordsworth's choice of subject that he wrote to him to express his disapproval. Wordsworth's response is instructive. Reflecting on true, authentic humanity, he asks,

> But where are we to find the best measure of this? I answer, from within; by stripping our own hearts naked, and by looking out of ourselves toward men who lead the simplest lives most according to nature men who have never known false refinements, wayward and artificial desires, false criticisms, effeminate habits of thinking and feeling, or who, having known these things, have outgrown them. This latter class is the most to be depended upon, but it is very small in number. People in our rank in life are perpetually falling into one sad mistake, namely, that of

supposing that human nature and the persons they associate with are one and the same thing. Whom do we generally associate with? Gentlemen, persons of fortune, professional men, ladies persons who can afford to buy or can easily procure books of half a guinea price, hot-pressed, and printed upon superfine paper. These persons are, it is true, a part of human nature, but we err lamentably if we suppose them to be fair representatives of the vast mass of human existence.[6]

In short, Wordsworth considers the idiot boy to be a purer, more authentic example of human nature precisely because he is not shaped or influenced by the corrupting nature of sophisticated society. We might say today that he has "no filters" and that with him, "what you see is what you get." His outward behavior is a precise reflection of his inner life. And he is also one who lives much closer to nature. He is, in fact, an example of that noble savage that is typically seen as the epitome of Rousseau's ideal human being.

In short, the Romantics grant an authority to feelings, to that inner psychological space, that all human beings possess. And those feelings are first and foremost genuine, pristine, and true guides to who human beings are. It is only society, with its petty rivalries, its competitiveness, and its artificial sophistication, that twists, perverts, and distorts those feelings. That is a key move in the path to the modern self, made more compelling by the fact that it is expressed in an artistic form rather than a philosophical argument.

Conclusion

Few today will have read Rousseau, if they have even heard of him. Perhaps a few more will have encountered the work of the great Romantic poets, though they are scarcely household names, and it is hard to imagine that many people build their philosophies of life around their works. So what is their significance for the narrative of the modern self?

They are important because they represent an impulse in the modern world that tends to see sophisticated society as corrupting and to regard instinct, or that inner voice of nature, as possessing significant authority. This may be an intuition in contemporary society, something we simply feel rather than upon which we consciously reflect. But it is all around us and lies behind the way in which authenticity has become a dominant theme in attitudes to what constitutes personal integrity. And because this is now a social or cultural intuition, it is helpful to look at those who have consciously reflected on and articulated it as a philosophy of life. Fish swim in water; they do not give it a second thought; but the scientist who analyzes water is far more informed about the aquatic environment. Thus, looking at Rousseau and the Romantics allows us to see the significance, and the tacit assumptions, of the culture in which we live.

Given all this, we can see why the foul-mouthed politician has supplanted the polite and reserved one, because in a world where the inner voice is key to the real person, the former is authentic while the latter presents a public image likely at odds with his private behavior. More pointedly, the trans person who was born male but claims to be a woman is to be lionized because that is an act of courage and honesty whereby the outward performance is finally brought into line with the inner reality, despite what society might say about such. All of this derives from authorizing—indeed, valorizing—that inner voice of nature and then expecting or even demanding that the outside world, from the public square to the individual's body, conform to this.

And yet Rousseau and the Romantics do not offer us a framework for understanding all aspects of the current manifestations of expressive individualism. For them, there was such a thing as human nature, and that meant that the inner voice of nature had a stable framework that transcended that of the individual. We might say that they regarded human nature not simply as, say, a biological phenomenon, a collection of matter organized according to certain genomic principles whereby a man could reproduce with a woman but not with a turtle or a chimpanzee. No, they also saw human nature as possessing a moral structure, something that all human beings share. So a return to authentic human nature meant a return to authentic human moral intuitions of empathy and sympathy—all of which would be shared in common. Rousseau's voice of nature would be the same as Shelley's and the same as yours and mine. They did not see their emphasis upon human subjectivity as leading to moral relativism and transforming ethics into matters of mere personal taste. The inner voice of nature was just that—the inner voice of *human* nature, a human nature with a moral structure that was shared by all.

Yet the modern imagination is infused with the rejection of the notion of human nature as imposing some kind of external moral authority upon us. Cultural relativism is the order of the day. And we are intuitively uncomfortable with, even offended by, the idea that one group in society might be able to object to the way in which another group conceptualizes or understands happiness. To understand the philosophical significance of those intuitions, it is helpful now to turn to the nineteenth century and to the work of two of its philosophers whose thought came to dominate elite intellectual circles in the West: Karl Marx and Friedrich Nietzsche.

Study Questions

1. In what ways might you be an expressive individualist?

2. How do you see original sin in the world today?

3. How is the inward reflection of the Psalms and Paul different from expressive individualism?

4. How is Wordsworth's "idiot boy" representative of expressive individualism?

3

Prometheus Unbound

Introduction

If one of the elements of the modern self—the significant authority that we now give to our inner feelings with regard to our identity—has precedent in the work of Rousseau and the Romantics, it is still clear that the story cannot stop there. The modern self is not simply one that sees inner feelings as authoritative; the modern self also largely rejects the idea that human nature has any intrinsic moral structure or significance. While we accept that there is a biological phenomenon that we might call human nature, something that means we cannot, for example, reproduce with lizards or chimpanzees, we tend not to draw any great moral implications from this. To assert, therefore, that human beings by their very nature should not engage in certain sexual practices is something unlikely to meet with popular affirmation today. The idea that merely being a human carries an intrinsic morality and moral purpose is seen as a fiction, and often regarded as one confected in order to justify the exploitation of one group by another.

These modern aspects of selfhood—the rejection of human nature as having a moral structure and the related belief that moral codes are inherently oppressive—find profound theoretical expression in the thought of two nineteenth-century figures in particular: Karl Marx and Friedrich Nietzsche. As with Rousseau and the Romantics, few today may have read them, but we all live in a world where many of their basic ideas are now our cultural intuitions.

From Hegel to Marx

Karl Marx emerged from a philosophical milieu in which the thought of G. W. F. Hegel was the dominant influence. While Hegel's thought is complicated, and typically expressed in difficult vocabulary, at its heart lies a relatively straightforward and important idea: human self-consciousness (i.e., how human beings think about themselves and the world around them) changes over time. The ancient Athenian thought differently from the medieval knight, who thought differently from the Prussian merchants of Hegel's own day. For Hegel, this process was one driven by ideas. In engaging with each other, humans found that the way they thought was transformed through this interaction.

This makes intuitive sense. If we reflect on our own lives, it should be obvious that who we are—how we think, the language we use, the way we interpret certain situations, the manner in which we respond to others—is intimately connected to the other people with whom we interact. Our self-consciousness is shaped by the way in which it engages with the self-consciousnesses of others, and vice versa. These interactions are dynamic and have an effect on us. Thus, we change over time. While I still have the same fingerprints I had as a child, I am in a sense quite a different person from the one who emerged from my mother's womb. And that raises the question of what exactly are we to understand by human nature. We might perhaps identify it with a biological thing, say, a certain genetic pattern that all human beings share; but that would be a very minimal definition and certainly does not address what it means to be an actual human being—a living, breathing, self-conscious individual capable of making decisions and moving intentionally into the future. The real question of human nature goes beyond basic biology; it really demands that we address questions of, say, morality and purpose. Does human nature carry with it a moral structure and a specific end or purpose that remain constant over time and to which we must conform ourselves in order to flourish? Or are we simply the stuff of which we are made and beyond that free to be or do whatever we so choose? Pieces of living playdough attached to a will? Once Hegel placed human self-consciousness at the center and observed how this changes over time, the question of this deeper sense of human nature became far more urgent.

We might summarize Hegel by saying that he saw true, full human nature as something emerging over time, as something to be realized by a historical process that would terminate at some point in the future. This process was one that he characterized as being one of Spirit. Again, Hegel's thinking about Spirit is complicated, but for our purposes here, it is simply important to note that he saw this process of the Spirit as driven by ideas. It was as self-consciousnesses interacted that ways of thinking were changed. This is where Marx both borrowed from, and rejected, Hegel. Indeed, in a backhanded compliment to his philosophical mentor, Marx declared that his own system turned Hegel on his head—which, as he wryly commented, was to turn him the right way up.

The key to understanding the particulars of Marx's own understanding of human nature lies in grasping the foundational concepts of his thought. While Hegel is what we call an idealist and interested in the intellectual spirit of the age (i.e., the ideas that gave it its distinctive shape), Marx is a materialist, and that in a twofold sense. He believes that the world is all that there is, that there is no transcendent realm, no God or gods behind this material universe that might provide a sacred foundation for any moral order. But Marx's materialism goes further: he believes that the material conditions of life, specifically the economic relations that exist between people, decisively shape how we think of reality. In short, it is those economic relations that have the most profound impact upon our self-consciousness and our identity. This also means that how we think about reality changes over time because economic relations change.

One implication of this understanding of human identity and relationships is that all forms of human community become political. Everything, from the village sports team to trade unions, draws its ultimate significance from the role it plays in the economic (and thus political) nature of society.

Another foundational concept, at least for the thought of the early Marx as expressed in what are now called his *Economic and Philosophical Manuscripts of 1844*, is that of *alienation*. Alienation at its simplest refers to that feeling that leaves us at odds with our surroundings. An example might be the experience many have in the school playground when they find themselves excluded from a game or from a group to which they wish to belong. The result is an unpleasant feeling of what we might describe as psychological or emotional discomfort.

For Marx, alienation is specifically connected (as the first point above would imply) to human beings in relation to economic considerations. A man feels alienation because he is alienated from the fruits of his labor. For example, he works long hours in a furniture factory, doing repetitive work such as hammering a nail into a piece of wood being passed down a production line and being paid a wage that barely allows him to feed and clothe his family. And he never enjoys the fruits of his labor. He never owns one of the chairs he makes. He never has the satisfaction of relaxing in one at the end of the workday. He is nothing more than a cog in a giant industrial machine. We might say such work is soul-destroying. Marx would say that it is alienating. It prevents men and women from being who they should be.

Marx's Critique of Religion

Alienation provides the background to Marx's critique of religion. As a man of the Enlightenment, he has no doubt that religion is false and that the Christian God does not exist. The work of previous thinkers, such as David Hume, has demonstrated that to his satisfaction. What interests Marx, therefore, is not the question of whether religion is true but rather why people persist in believing that it is true long after it has ceased to be a valid intellectual option. This question Marx resolves psychologically, building on the work of a contemporary materialist philosopher, Ludwig Feuerbach.

In an important work, *The Essence of Christianity*, Feuerbach offered an account of religion in strictly materialist terms that Marx found compelling. Here is a key passage:

> Religion, at least the Christian, is the relation of man to himself, or more correctly to his own nature (i.e., his subjective nature); but a relation of it, viewed as a nature apart from his own. The divine being is nothing else than the human being, or, rather, the human nature purified, freed from the limits of the individual

man, made objective—i.e., contemplated and revered as another, a distinct being. All the attributes of the divine nature are, therefore, attributes of the human nature.[1]

What Feuerbach is saying here is that religious talk about God—talk that a believer thinks is referring to God as an objective being—is really just talk about humanity, an ideal version but humanity nonetheless, projected onto an idea that has no real existence. We might put this in more accessible terms by saying that God-talk really represents wishful thinking on humanity's part. And the reason human beings do this is because they are alienated. They know they are not what they should be, and so they relieve their frustration by inventing a being called God, onto whom they place their ideals, hopes, and aspirations.

Marx picks up on Feuerbach's critique of religion. He agrees that it is a function of alienation, but he develops it in two specific ways. First, consistent with his emphasis on economic relations as foundational to who we are and how we think, he sees religion as deriving from economic conditions. As a result, religious teachings must be understood in terms of those economic conditions. Religion may make claims about something spiritual and otherworldly, but it is really this world that is its primary concern. Thus, for Marx, religious morality is really an expression of the economic concerns of the dominant class; in the case of nineteenth-century Europe, this was the bourgeoisie—the factory owners, the merchants, the middle class.

Take, for example, Christianity's teaching, taught from myriad pulpits over the years, that husbands and wives should be faithful to each other, should not drink too much, and should work hard and honestly for their masters or employers. A Christian might see these as imperatives because they are the will of God and the means by which human beings, made in his image, can flourish. Marx, however, would see such a belief as mystical nonsense. For him, these imperatives are the means by which the middle-class employers make sure that their workers are the kind of people who make up a stable, sober, obedient workforce. And he would interpret the grounding of these imperatives in religious arguments simply as a manipulative way of granting them an absolute moral authority that cannot be challenged. That which is convenient, even necessary, for maintaining the world of the factory owner is disguised as a nonnegotiable imperative rooted in the character and command of God.

Marx's second development from Feuerbach is even more radical. Philosophers like Feuerbach merely describe the world; for Marx, the purpose of philosophy is to change it. To put it bluntly: if religion is one major means by which the current unjust set of economic relations is maintained, then at the heart of any drive to transform society must lie a pungent and effective criticism of religion. As Marx himself puts it in a famous passage on the nature of religion,

> The foundation of irreligious criticism is: Man makes religion, religion does not make man. Religion is indeed the self-consciousness and self-esteem of man who has either not yet won through to himself or has already lost himself again. . . . The struggle against religion is therefore indirectly the struggle against that world whose spiritual aroma is religion.
>
> Religious suffering is at one and the same time the expression of real suffering and a protest against real suffering. Religion is the sigh of the oppressed creature, the heart of a heartless world and the soul of soulless conditions. It is the opium of the people.

The abolition of religion as the illusory happiness of the people
is the demand for their real happiness.[2]

We should note three things here. First, Marx regards religion as
a human creation with no transcendent status and no necessarily
abiding significance. At its most positive, religion fills a psychological need: the pain and suffering that economic alienation causes
are alleviated by the false hope of a life of eternal bliss hereafter,
where all wrongs are righted and peace and justice prevail. Second,
this not only meets the psychological needs of the workers but also
works in the interests of the bosses and factory owners because it
enables them to bear their present woes and not rise up in rebellion.
Third, this means that the demolition of false hope—the debunk-
ing of religion—is vital if the working class is to realize the truly
desperate nature of its condition and then take action in this world
to rectify the situation.

In short, Marx lays the groundwork for some of the most basic
of our culture's contemporary intuitions: Religion is a sign of intellectual weakness in its adherents and a means of social oppression
for its proponents. Further, freedom can be achieved only by the
abolition of religion. Above all, the idea that human nature is to be
morally framed by theological claims such as the notion that men
and women are made in the image of God is to be repudiated. Of
course, few today have read Marx himself, but these ideas have in
many ways infiltrated the cultural imagination in which religion
is instinctively regarded as both childish and oppressive.

We should also notice in closing that Marx's claim that all human
social relations are economic relations has one more significant
result: all human social relations must therefore be political because
they all serve the status quo. Whether we are talking about Boy

Scouts or the local golf club, in Marx's world all have political significance. If society itself is to be transformed, then these too must be arenas of political combat. That probably sounds very familiar in a world where the last decade has seen cake baking, flower arranging, and school bathroom policies subjected to acrimonious legal wrangling. The prepolitical is no more. There is nothing in this world where human beings can relate to each other that is not a potential arena of political conflict, because all areas of life connect to the overall economic structure of society and thus to society's inequalities and injustices; and Marx should be given much of the credit for laying the theoretical foundations of that.

Friedrich Nietzsche and the Death of God

Like Marx, Nietzsche both assumes that the Enlightenment's demolition of the Christian faith was decisive and yet is fascinated by the fact that religion persists as a reality in society and in people's individual lives. And, again like Marx, he is interested in a psychological explanation for this. And even though his answer differs from that of the communist philosopher in important ways, his ideas too have become part of the intuitive nature of our surrounding culture.

Nietzsche is not simply interested in why religion persists. He is also fascinated by the fact that the influence of religion persists even among those who have come to reject its central claims, such as the existence of God. This is clear from two famous passages in his major work, *The Gay Science* (or, *The Joyful Wisdom*). In the first, he recounts a legend about the Buddha:

> After Buddha was dead, his shadow was still shown for centuries in a cave—a tremendous, gruesome shadow. God is dead; but

given the way of men, there may still be caves for thousands of years in which his shadow will be shown. And we—we still have to vanquish his shadow too.[3]

Nietzsche's point is that the power of Buddha persisted long after his death, and that not in a good way. The image of a gruesome shadow summons up something oppressive and frightening. But, of course, it is not the power of Buddha with which Nietzsche is concerned. Rather, it is the ongoing power of God, who has been successfully slain as a plausible idea by the philosophers of the Enlightenment but who continues to exert an oppressive and ominous influence on the way people think and societies are organized. But Nietzsche's most dramatic statement of this comes some paragraphs later, in a passage that really must be quoted at length:

The madman.—Have you not heard of that madman who lit a lantern in the bright morning hours, ran to the market place, and cried incessantly: "I seek God! I seek God." As many of those who did not believe in God were standing around just then, he provoked much laughter. Has he got lost? Asked one. Did he lose his way like a child? Asked another. Or is he hiding? Is he afraid of us? Has he gone on a voyage? Emigrated?—Thus they yelled and laughed.

The madman jumped into their midst and pierced them with his eyes. "Whither is God?" he cried: "I will tell you. We have killed him—you and I. All of us are his murderers. But how did we do this? How could we drink up the sea? Who gave us the sponge to wipe away the entire horizon? What were we doing when we unchained this earth from its sun? Whither is it moving now? Whither are we moving? Away from all suns? Are we not plunging continually? Backward, sideward, forward, in all directions? Is there still any up or down? Are we not straying as through an infinite nothing? Do we not feel the breath of empty space? Has it not become colder? Is not night continually closing in on us? Do we not need to light lanterns in the morning? Do we hear nothing as yet of the noise of the gravediggers who are burying God? Do we smell nothing as yet of the divine decomposition? Gods too decompose. God is dead. God remains dead. And we have killed him.

"How shall we comfort ourselves, the murderers of all murderers? What was holiest and mightiest of all that the world has yet owned has bled to death under our knives: who will wipe this blood off us? What water is there for us to clean ourselves? What festivals of atonement, what sacred games shall we have to invent? Is not the greatness of this deed too great for us? Must we ourselves not become gods simply to appear worthy of it? There has never been a greater deed; and whoever is born after us—for the sake of this deed he will belong to a higher history than all history hitherto."[4]

The passage is perhaps most famous for the phrase "God is dead," repeated from the aphorism about the Buddha. Nietzsche chose the phrase carefully: God has not simply become irrelevant or implausible over time. Enlightenment philosophy has intentionally denied his relevance and even his existence. It has done away with him. But here is the rub: Enlightenment philosophers have failed to draw the necessary conclusions from this notion. Thus, a figure like the great Immanuel Kant constructed a philosophy in which God played no direct role but was still necessary as the presupposition of morality. That is precisely the kind of philosopher Nietzsche's

Madman here challenges. What he is in effect saying is: You cannot dispense with God, or shove him to margins, or make him nothing more than a necessary presupposition for morality. If you displace God, if you kill him, then everything changes. Nothing, absolutely nothing, can stay the same. Most pointedly, there is no moral stability to the universe. There is nothing greater to which the individual must, or even can, be held accountable. There is no moral structure to human nature, no "end" in light of which all human beings should shape and direct their lives. We are free from all such constraints.

We might say that the death of God is also the death of human nature, or at least the end of any cogent argument that there is such a thing as human nature. If there is no God, then men and women cannot be made in his image and are not therefore required to act in accordance with that image. And if men and women are not made in God's image, to what absolute moral standard must they submit themselves? To none, says Nietzsche, for the very idea of an absolute moral standard becomes meaningless in a world that is intrinsically of no significance beyond the matter from which it is made.

The Nature of Morality

If the death of God means the death of human nature and of any absolute moral standard, then what is morality? Here, Nietzsche offers a line of reasoning that is analogous to that of Marx: morality is manipulative, a way of one person or group exerting power over another, covering this manipulation with the veneer of transcendent authority. And typically it is the weak and the despicable—in Nietzsche's view, those who are unwilling or unable to rise to the challenge of self-creation—that indulge in such things. Thus, the claim that, say, stealing or killing is wrong because it is against God's will is simply a way of the weak turning the strength of those capable of taking what they want into a vice or a sin. Nietzsche expresses this in terms of a linguistic switch. Originally, he says, there were the ideas of good and bad. Good meant strength, bad meant weakness. But over time, and largely through the influence of Christianity and what he dubbed its "slave morality," strength became identified with evil and weakness with good. The result was that what was once considered to be good has come to be seen as evil; and what was once considered bad has come to be seen as good. When Christianity put forth a God whose strength was made perfect in weakness, it provided a specious rationale for making this inversion, for glorifying weakness and despising strength. As with Marx, Nietzsche sees religion's continued existence in the modern world as something to be explained in psychological terms. This persistence of belief in God fulfills a twofold function: it is a crutch or an excuse by which the weak can avoid the challenge of creating their own meaning in an otherwise meaningless universe; and it is a means by which the weak can demonize and manipulate the strong.

For Nietzsche, then, the great task facing human beings is to break free of the metaphysical myths that religion weaves and to shatter the moral codes that hinder individuals from being strong. We might express Nietzsche's thought this way: freed from the burden of being creatures of God, human beings must rise to the challenge of self-creation, of being whoever they choose to be. Put perhaps even more bluntly: be whoever or whatever works for you. You should feel no obligation to conform to the standards or criteria of anybody else.

So what criteria should we use, according to Nietzsche, to discern what actions are good and what are bad? Well, at the heart of

Nietzsche's approach is self-creation: if there is no God, then we are our own masters. We might put it another way, using an analogy of which Nietzsche himself is fond: we are artists and, as such, we are tasked with the art of self-creation. We might put this in more familiar terms: we are to be whatever we want or choose to be. Whatever makes us feel good about ourselves, that is what we should do. The language of morality is really a way of hiding the fact that that is what the culturally powerful are already doing: when they tell us this action is right or that action is wrong, they are really saying this action is something they like and that is something they do not like. They are simply giving their personal tastes, the things that they find helpful and convenient, the things that keep them in positions of power and influence, a veneer of transcendent authority.

Nietzsche's notion that morality is really about taste is very helpful in thinking about our current moral climate. So often the language we use confirms that Nietzsche's perspective is now a cultural intuition. So often we will speak of morality in terms of taste or aesthetics: "That remark was hurtful;" "That idea is offensive;" "That viewpoint makes me feel unsafe." Notice that such expressions do not make a statement about whether the matters in hand are right or wrong. In fact, the underlying assumption is that the offensiveness or hurtfulness of them is identical with the moral content. The subjective response has become the ethical criterion for judgment. We shall return to this point in chapter 8.

The Superman

The shattering of the bondage of the old religious and metaphysical morality is epitomized in Nietzsche's concept of the superman, a figure to which he points in several works as one who transcends the rather pitiful kind of humanity of Nietzsche's own day. Unfortunately, the idea has been somewhat obscured by the association in the popular mind of Nietzsche with German Nazism. It is therefore often connected to a notion of the "Master Race." As Nietzsche himself was critical of both German nationalism and anti-Semitism, however, any identification of the superman with some kind of Aryan stormtrooper is therefore misplaced. The superman is rather the one who engages in dramatic, transgressive self-creation.

Goethe, the great German polymath, probably represents for Nietzsche himself the closest thing to the superman: a free spirit who transcended the spirit of his own age, a man of both intellectual brilliance and significant action. But I would like to suggest that another perhaps represents this type as well, and this a figure who in many ways is the harbinger of much that characterizes our present age: Oscar Wilde.

The cultural historian Modris Eksteins sees Wilde as the quintessential figure of modernity because the kind of self-expressive rebellion that Nietzsche envisaged finds its most obvious manifestation in the shattering of traditional codes of sexual morality. Rebellion in our modern world is intimately connected to sexual iconoclasm. And Wilde is central to this. As Eksteins comments,

> The sexual rebel, particularly the homosexual, became a central figure in the imagery of revolt, especially after the ignominious treatment Oscar Wilde received at the hands of the establishment.[5]

The rebellious Nietzschean impulse is found in three particular aspects of Wilde's life and thought. First, the artist is the greatest exemplar of how life should be lived because the artist creates and performs; he does not simply conform to the crowd or, as

Nietzsche might have expressed it, to "the morality of the herd."[6]
As Wilde declares,

> Most people are other people. Their thoughts are someone else's
> opinions, their lives a mimicry, their passions a quotation.[7]

Ironically, he makes this statement during an extended reflection
on the significance of Christ. But Christ's significance for Wilde is
not that ascribed to him by orthodox Christianity. Rather, it is the
fact that Christ is the supreme individualist, the one who breaks
with the social conventions and expectations of his day to tread his
own intentional path through the world. The call here is for the
individual to break with the herd and be a self-creator, something
that Wilde did with relish, from his stylish clothes to his legendary
witticisms to his sexual adventurism. In his defiance of convention, it is easy to see an adumbration of the kind of outrageous
behavior that our world of reality TV has made virtually normative. We might even say that Wilde's rebellion against the spirit of
his (Victorian) age has become the spirit of our own modern age.

The second Nietzschean element we find in Wilde is the notion
that art should be detached from any kind of moral code. In the
preface to his most famous work, *The Picture of Dorian Gray*, he
makes the following observations:

> There is no such thing as a moral or an immoral book.
> Books are well-written or badly written. That is all.[8]

In saying this, Wilde is striking against the Victorian notion that
literature should be morally improving to those who read it. For him,
by contrast, the purpose is a purely aesthetic one and, as becomes

clear in responses to critical reviews of his book, one that is actually focused merely on the pleasure of the artist, not his audience:

> I wrote this book entirely for my own pleasure, and it gave me very great pleasure to write it. Whether it becomes popular or not is a matter of absolute indifference to me.[9]

Wilde reiterates this view in his essay *The Soul of Man Under Socialism*:

> A true artist takes no notice whatever of the public. The public are to him non-existent.[10]

In short, art is for art's sake; indeed, art is for the artist's sake. The act of artistic creation is that which gives the artist pleasure, and that is an end in itself.

This leads to the third aspect of Wilde that is Nietzschean: ethics is really aesthetics, or a matter of taste. This is Nietzsche's conclusion, given the death of God and the absence of any external authority upon which an ethical code can be built. What is good and what is evil is simply a matter of the tastes or preferences of those with power and, indeed, the means by which they maintain their power. In Wilde, this switch from the language of ethics to the language of taste is explicit and self-conscious. And the key to this is human freedom: the actions of the individual are governed by the idea of personal, creative freedom, a point Wilde makes explicit in *The Soul of Man Under Socialism*:

> A man cannot always be estimated by what he does. He may keep the law, and yet be worthless. He may break the law, and

yet be fine. He may be bad, without ever doing anything bad. He may commit a sin against society, and yet realize through that sin his true perfection.[11]

Here, actions cease to have intrinsic moral value; what makes them "moral'" rather is the freedom with which they are performed. Wilde sees marriage as an institution that should fall because it imposes external limits on the individual's ability to act on desire. Indeed, the whole idea of some external, objectively valid morality must be erased. As Wilde says, all that matters is whether a person "realizes the perfection of the soul that is within him. All imitation in morals and life is wrong."[12]

Notice that last sentence—"all imitation in morals and life is wrong." In short, free, artistic creation of the self is the only moral criterion and imperative. Spontaneity, transgression, and self-expression are the core of Wilde's (and Nietzsche's) philosophy of life, a philosophy in which what is aesthetically pleasing has supplanted the notion of moral correctness.

Conclusion

Several points of significance for today emerge from an examination of the thought of Marx, Nietzsche, and Wilde. Marx's distinctive contribution is arguably the way in which his claim that human social relations are at root economic relations leads to the conclusion that all things are therefore political. To put this another way, it leads to the abolition of the prepolitical because all forms of social organization have significance in serving the existing structure of society. This is why our current world is characterized by battles over such things as the Boy Scouts, cake baking, and school uniforms. On this front, Marx has won, for as soon as one side in the cultural conflict politicizes an institution, the other side has no choice but to engage on those terms. We are all, in a sense, Marxists now.

While Marx is in many ways a very different philosopher from Nietzsche, the two men share a common rejection of the idea that human beings as human beings have a transcendent, stable, moral nature to which they need to conform in order to flourish. For Marx, morality is historically conditioned and designed to justify and maintain the current (unjust) economic structure of society. For Nietzsche, morality is a fiction invented by one group to denigrate and subordinate another. For both, moral codes are thus manipulative and must be transgressed to find true freedom. The same applies therefore to religion. While Marx will allow religion a certain analgesic function for those suffering in this life, both he and Nietzsche see it as something that is at best a crutch, at worst a manipulative confidence trick designed to prevent people from being truly themselves.

And for Nietzsche, those "selves" are to be found through artistic self-creation that defies convention or herd morality and strikes out on its own, daring to take the role left vacant by the death of God. And in Oscar Wilde, we find the classic, sophisticated example of what that might look like: the transgressive, sexual adventurer, for whom pleasure was an end in itself, and for whom aesthetics replaced the outmoded and oppressive notion of an external moral code.

In this regard, all three men point to something that is now a basic assumption of our modern cultural imagination: there is little or no moral structure to human nature. To be human is merely to be an intentional thinking agent. What we think and what we do is our business, as we are not answerable to any higher power or even to the authority of our own bodies. We can be whoever we want to be and act however we want to act. Morality, if it features at all, is something that is contextually determined. For example, did that person consent to the sexual act in which the two of us engaged? The act itself has no moral significance beyond that.

We shall return to each of these themes later, but it is worth noting here that the turn to art and self-creation, or self-expression, runs deep in contemporary culture. Social media has allowed lives to become acts of public performance. And it is surely remarkable how much slack we allow to artists with regard to personal morality. Prior to #MeToo, Hollywood celebrities made it a virtual annual tradition to complain that Roman Polanski, convicted child rapist, was banned from the United States and thus from the Oscars ceremony. We might also note how moral iconoclasm is the standard métier of the creative classes in our society. And that iconoclasm is, as it was for Wilde, frequently and most prominently sexual in character. Which brings us to the topic of our next chapter: the way in which sex and politics became so intertwined in the twentieth century.

Study Questions

1. How might a Christian respond to Marx's idea of alienation?

2. What can we learn from Nietzsche's Madman?

3. How is Oscar Wilde a harbinger of our present age?

4

Sexualizing Psychology, Politicizing Sex

Introduction

One of the most obvious aspects of modern public life is the central role that sex plays within it. This should strike us as rather odd: the fact that the most private and intimate act between two people has become so important to public life is surely a strange development. Indeed, from legislation on matters such as gay marriage through to the apparent need of the public to know about the sexual orientation of sports stars and actors, the role of sex in our culture is pervasive and arguably unprecedented. Why should this be the case?

The simple answer is that sexual desire has emerged in the last one hundred years as a primary category for understanding our identity. In biblical times or in ancient Greece, sex was regarded as something that human beings *did*; today it is considered to be something vital to who human beings *are*. Hence, we now have the whole notion of sexual identity and the ever-expanding letters that make up the LGBTQ+ alliance.

How has this development taken place? A complete answer, of course, would need to address all manner of social and cultural developments, from the advent of technology to the crumbling authority of traditional institutions such as the church. We will touch a little on these in chapters 5 and 6. First, however, let us look at the thinkers who helped to shape the theoretical basis of the modern political discourse on sex and sexuality.

Sigmund Freud and Human Happiness

The single most important figure in the intellectual story is Sigmund Freud. Today, it is true that many of his psychoanalytic theories have been discredited. The notion of the Oedipus complex, for example, is widely dismissed as a fiction. But his legacy lives on in two important areas: his notion that sex is foundational to human happiness and his theory of civilization.

First, the notion that sex is foundational to human happiness is central to Freud's thinking. Happiness is, of course, a basic human desire and something that has often been regarded as part of the purpose of a life well lived. Aristotle saw it as embodied in a life lived according to virtue. Christians have typically seen it as the result of a life ordered to glorifying God. In the Declaration of Independence, Thomas Jefferson listed the pursuit of happiness as one of three basic, natural, God-given rights, along with life and liberty, that all human beings should possess. We might say that for Aristotle, for Christians, and for Jefferson, the question of happiness is central to the question of human ends and central to the notion of human nature. Indeed, it is a vital part of what it means to be human.

With the collapse of the belief in human nature as possessing an intrinsic moral structure, to which Marx's and Nietzsche's thought witnessed, the question of happiness becomes a matter of serious contention. What exactly does it look like? Can different people think of their end, and thus of what happiness is, in different ways? Does happiness have a stable core of content, or is it an entirely subjective matter, varying from person to person?

Now, while Freud abandons the notion of human nature as having an intrinsic moral structure, he does believe that human beings still share something in common. Here he builds on a longstanding Enlightenment tradition of seeing pleasure and pain as central to thinking about good and evil, happiness and the lack thereof:

> What do [people] demand of life and wish to achieve in it? The answer to this can hardly be in doubt. They strive after happiness; they want to become happy and to remain so. This endeavor has two sides, a positive and a negative aim. It aims, on the one hand, at an absence of pain and unpleasure, and, on the other, at the experiencing of strong feelings of pleasure.[1]

So, seeking pleasure and avoiding pain are key to the definition of happiness. And where is the greatest pleasure to be found? Freud is in no doubt:

> Man's discovery that sexual (genital) love afforded him the strongest experiences of satisfaction and in fact provided him with the prototype of all happiness, must have suggested to him that he should continue to seek the satisfaction of happiness in his life along the path of sexual relations and that he should make genital erotism the central point of his life.[2]

This is a very important point. If the fundamental form of human happiness is the genital pleasure derived from sex, then we can conclude that for Freud human nature is at its deepest level sexual and that human beings are therefore defined in a basic way by their sexual desires. When we add to this that Freud also saw sexual desire as existing from infancy, the point is further reinforced: our identities as human beings are in a very important sense fundamentally defined by our sexual desires.

It is difficult to overestimate the importance of this move to make sexual desire central to human identity. In modern society, everything from the common use of terms such as "straight" and "gay" in everyday conversation to the underlying assumptions of international human rights law presuppose that this is the case. And the idea that human flourishing is virtually synonymous with sexual fulfillment is a commonplace—in fact, virtually an intuition—of modern Western culture. The fulfilled life is a sexually fulfilled life. That is the unmistakable message projected from a myriad of commercials, sitcoms, soap operas, and movies. Pornography is big business, and of massive economic significance. Sex counseling is a booming industry. Drugs designed to preserve the libido into old age are now a basic part of health care. Modern culture's portrayal of traditional sexual standards—virginity, chastity, modesty, even monogamy—is typically engineered to present these values as somehow inadequate, even oppressive and dehumanizing. And Freud is the man who originally expressed this understanding of human happiness in a cogent, plausible, scientific form. As the abolition of the prepolitical makes us all Marxists now, so the assumption that sex is happiness makes us all Freudians.

Freud, Morality, and Civilization

If sex is basic to what it means to be a human being, the question obviously arises: Why, then, does society typically place so many restrictions on sexual behavior? Freud's answer has two dimensions: he sees morality at root as conventional, as a matter of cultural practices, and not as grounded in some larger, objective moral structure of nature; and he sees moral conventions as serving to create and maintain civilization.

As to the first, the following comment makes the point clear. Talking about sexual activities that societies have condemned (e.g., homosexuality), he declares,

> Those who condemn the other [sexual] practices (which have no doubt been common among mankind from primeval times) as being perversions, are giving way to an unmistakable feeling of disgust, which protects them from accepting sexual aims of the kind. The limits of such disgust are, however, often purely conventional: a man who will kiss a pretty girl's lips passionately, may perhaps be disgusted at the idea of using her toothbrush, though there are no grounds for supposing that his own oral cavity, for which he feels no disgust, is any cleaner than the girl's. Here, then, our attention is drawn to the factor of disgust, which interferes with the libidinal over-valuation of the sexual object but can in turn be overridden by libido. Disgust seems to be one of the forces which have led to a restriction of the sexual aim.[3]

Freud's argument is rather clever: morality rests on notions of disgust, cultivated in the individual by the wider culture, in order to provoke revulsion at certain behaviors. But the basis for that revulsion is not rational. It is merely that of a social convention. A man might object to using his girlfriend's toothbrush ostensibly on grounds of hygiene; but he will rather enjoy giving her a passionate kiss that involves the same compromise of his personal cleanliness.

And so, Freud argues, morality is really a matter of cultural tastes. In this, we might see him as standing in line with Nietzsche and Wilde, who also saw ethical claims as actually aesthetic statements dressed up in the language of objective morality.

As with Freud's notion that sex is identity, a case can be made for saying that the idea of morality as taste is now intuitive to Western society. Think of the language we routinely use in everyday conversation to express moral judgment: "I don't like that." "That behavior disgusts me." "That was a tasteless joke." "I find your argument offensive." "That was a hurtful comment." "I felt unsafe in that classroom discussion." These statements are aesthetic in the sense that they are rooted in feelings or sentiments. We may well think we are talking about right and wrong, truth and falsehood, but the change in vocabulary is significant. After all, a statement can be hurtful or offensive but still be true. "Trueman, you are bald and have crooked teeth" would be one that comes immediately to my own mind. Offensive. Hurtful even. But sadly, very true. Yet increasingly, we conflate the hurtful with the wrong and the affirming with the truth. Our very language witnesses here to the collapsing of morality into questions of taste as shaped by the culture that surrounds us.

If Freud's analysis of the aesthetic aspect of morality invites obvious comparison with that of Nietzsche and Wilde, his understanding of what social function morality fulfills has affinities with that of Marx. For Marx, morality served to maintain the social order that best served the interests of the dominant economic class; in the case of nineteenth-century Britain, this means that of the bourgeoisie, of the middle class. For Freud, morality served to make human social life possible. Society has a vested interest in cultivating powerful moral instincts within us, such that we feel deep shame and guilt if we go against them, in order to preserve civilization. As Freud expresses the problem:

> Primitive man was better off in knowing no restrictions of instinct. To counterbalance this, his prospects of enjoying this happiness for any length of time were very slender. Civilized man has exchanged a portion of his possibilities of happiness for a portion of security.[4]

This passage is worth connecting to the earlier ideas of Rousseau that we examined in chapter 2. For Rousseau, human beings are most authentic when connected with the inner voice of nature. That is what makes them empathetic and promotes true morality. Polite society, with its conventions, its rivalries, and its petty jealousies, is what corrupts; only a return to that inner voice can truly make men and women authentically moral. But what if Freud is right? What if the inner voice of nature is not one that leads to empathy for other human beings but is rather a powerful sex drive that seeks sexual gratification? If that is the case, then allowing that inner voice to find outward expression will lead to a very different scenario, one that is dark and violent. In short, such a world would be one of social chaos, dominated by the most physically powerful males, for whom everybody else will simply be an instrumental object for the achievement of sexual pleasure.

To avoid this, society engages in a trade-off: it places restrictions on sexual desire through cultivating "morality"—a code of behavior by which guilt and shame about certain sexual behaviors are internalized. By so doing, this allows human beings to live together in some kind of social arrangement. This is what Freud calls "civilization" but what we might also call "culture." Sexual instincts are curbed, thwarted, and redirected so that men and women can live together with some degree of security.

This is where Freud's view of religion is significant. While Freud regards it as infantile, he does see it as fulfilling an important function: it provides a system for justifying the sexual codes necessary for the existence of civilization. Indeed, he declares that it "has clearly performed great services for human civilization. It has contributed much towards the taming of the asocial instincts."[5] Freud essentially says yes, religion is childish nonsense, but if people believe it, then it does at least offer a speciously transcendent basis for the sexual morality that keeps society civilized.

The drawback to civilization should be obvious at this point, given that it requires the frustration of natural sexual instincts. This means that there is a level of discontentment that then marks human existence: true happiness becomes unattainable precisely because the avenue to it—a sexual free-for-all—is precluded. Hence the title of Freud's monograph, *Civilization and Its Discontents*. And for Freud this is where cultural pursuits—art, music, sports, religion, etc.—come into play. They are ways of redirecting that sexual energy into activities that bring some satisfaction, even if it is not as great as that which untrammeled sex would provide. And it is this tension, this conflict, between human desire and the needs of civilization that is the point at which sex enters the political consciousness.

Sex Becomes Political

There is a sense in which sex has always been political. Sexual codes serve to define and delimit some of the most basic elements of any given society through their decisive connection to family and kinship relations. Thus, Menelaus launched a full-scale war against

Troy because Paris had stolen his wife; Mark Antony's affair with Cleopatra damaged his Roman power base and led to his fall; the English Reformation was triggered by the desire of the king to divorce and remarry in order to secure a male heir. Throughout history, sex has always been inextricably linked with politics.

The relationship of the two today, however, is more explicit and more omnipresent than in the past. It is now not so much the case that the desire to transgress society's traditional sexual codes poses a political challenge. It is that politics has become identified in many ways precisely with the overthrowal and reformulation of those codes. Sexual codes are now the material of political policy making in a way that the average Westerner in 1950 would have found incomprehensible, let alone the denizen of the world of Paris, Mark Antony, or Henry VIII.

Such a development was hardly surprising once the thinking of Freud took hold. If we are at root defined in large part by our sexual desires—if sexual desire (or "orientation," as we now say) is who we are—then sex must be political because rules governing sexual behavior are rules that govern what is and is not considered by society to be legitimate as an identity.

This self-conscious sexualizing of politics is, in terms of intellectual genealogy, largely the result of the fusion of certain elements of Marxist and Freudian thought in the 1930s. By that time, Marxism itself became something of a diverse and divided school of thought, with Leninists, Stalinists, and Trotskyists, among others, battling for the right to claim the legacy. Most significant for this narrative were events in Germany after the First World War. On paper, it should have been ripe for Marxist revolution: a highly developed industrial society that had just suffered devastating defeat in a war that had cost it dearly in terms of loss of life and economic power.

But the attempted workers' revolution of 1919 had failed, and the economic calamities of the 1920s had fueled the rise of militant right-wing nationalism. By the 1930s, many in the working class were supporting not the Marxist parties of the left but the nationalist parties of the right—most notably the National Socialists (Nazis). The question as to why the proletariat seemed to want to vote for politicians who would not serve their class interests was a pressing one for Marxist theory. And one figure who offered a most influential answer to this question was Wilhelm Reich, a young psychoanalyst who had been part of Freud's circle in Vienna but whom Freud himself came to regard as too extreme.

Wilhelm Reich: Where Marx Meets Freud

On the surface, Marx and Freud are not obvious bedfellows. Marx has an optimistic view of human society. Yes, the revolution will be painful, but ultimately human beings will be able to live in a non-alienated condition once the workers own the means of production. For Freud, however, our dark inner world of violent sexual desire means that there can never be a utopia, only societies with varying degrees of discontentment.

What Reich does to bring the two together, however, is use Marx's notion that human nature is an historical construct to make Freud's insights useful for Marxist thought. For example, he declares,

> It becomes apparent that it is not cultural activity itself which demands suppression and repression of sexuality, but only the present forms of this activity, and so one is willing to sacrifice these forms if by so doing the terrible wretchedness of children could be eliminated.[6]

What Reich means here is that it is not the idea of civilization or culture in the abstract, or as a universal phenomenon, that requires the kind of sexual codes we find in society. Rather, these forms, these codes, are historically contingent. We might recast this as follows: These particular sexual codes serve the purpose of maintaining this particular form of society or social organization. He agrees with Freud that sexual morality is the trade-off that society makes in order to be stable and secure. But the specific content of this trade-off is determined by the specific shape of the society in which it occurs.

Reich is a Marxist, so when he examines the sexual codes of his day, he is particularly sensitive to what he sees as the class interests that are protected or reinforced by sexual codes. In short, he views them as maintaining not simply civilization in general but specifically the kind of bourgeois, middle class, capitalist culture that German life embodies. In 1930s Germany, Reich sees these codes as reinforcing an institution that serves to cultivate a mindset with a tendency to follow authoritarian leadership figures. Again,

> The interlacing of the socio-economic structure with the sexual structure of society and the structural reproduction of society take place in the first four or five years and in the authoritarian family. The church only continues this function later. Thus, the authoritarian state gains an enormous interest in the authoritarian family. It becomes the factory in which the state's structure and ideology are moulded.[7]

In plain English, the sexual morality of Reich's day is designed to reinforce the structure and authority of the traditional family. The social function of the traditional family is to raise children who are instinctively obedient to a strong authoritarian (father) figure—in Reich's eyes, a figure such as Hitler. Reich continues,

> Morality's aim is to produce acquiescent subjects who, despite distress and humiliation, are adjusted to the authoritarian order. Thus, the family is the authoritarian state in miniature, to which the child must learn to adapt himself as a preparation for the general social adjustment required of him later.[8]

In this, Reich belongs to a long-standing tradition of suspicion or criticism of the traditional family as a norm. Rousseau abandoned all of his children to an orphanage on the self-serving ground that the orphanage would provide better for them than he could himself. William Godwin, the English radical thinker, attacked the idea of lifelong monogamy as oppressive and socially damaging, as did his son-in-law, the poet Percy Bysshe Shelley. Friedrich Engels, Marx's friend, patron, and collaborator, had written a substantial analysis and critique of the bourgeois family in its relationship to the development of private property. What Reich does is turn this tradition of critique in a psychological direction. This moves Marxism, and indeed the left, toward a new framework for understanding political oppression.

We can see this in the proposals Reich makes for what revolution might look like. In his most important work, *The Sexual Revolution*, he makes the point that Freud was correct in seeing the role of sexual repression as the basis for civilization but incorrect in generalizing this to all cultures and not simply that of societies built around the patriarchal family. Thus, revolution will involve the dismantling of the sexual codes on which the bourgeois family is built. In a frank passage, Reich declares,

The free society will provide ample room and security for the gratification of natural needs. Thus, it will not only not prohibit a love relationship between two adolescents of the opposite sex but will give it all manner of social support. Such a society will not only not prohibit the child's masturbation but, on the contrary, will probably conclude that any adult who hinders the development of the child's sexuality should be severely dealt with.[9]

The point is clear: sexual codes must be shattered if human beings are to be truly free. Those things that inhibit the free sexual expression, even of young children, are oppressive and prevent individuals from truly being themselves.

Of course, the question immediately rises of who exactly is going to facilitate this revolution in sexual codes if the family (and later the church) have a vested interest in maintaining the old, oppressive standards of behavior. The answer lies in the last sentence of the above quotation: society will do so, by promoting this sexual freedom and dealing severely with those who oppose it. In short, sex must become a pressing political issue in which the State takes a proactive interest. Reich writes this in the mid-1930s. No one who lives in the Western world today will find his statement to be anything less than prophetic. From teaching elementary school children about contraception and homosexuality onward, the state has arrogated to itself the policing of the education of children in sexual matters. And this is not a random development but one predicated on an assumption about the relationship of sex to personhood. To quote Reich,

The existence of strict moral principles has invariably signified that the biological, and specifically the sexual, needs of man were not being satisfied. Every moral regulation is in itself sex-negating, and all compulsory morality is life-negating. The social revolution has no more important task than finally to enable human beings to realize their full potentialities and find gratification in life.[10]

The implications of this are dramatic. For example, it turns on its head the traditional notion of education as the means by which the individual is formed by institutional authority to curb natural instincts in order to become an adult member of society. By contrast, this is Rousseau with a sexual twist: the authentic person is the sexual being, the one guided by the inner voice of (sexualized) nature, and the role of education is not to repress that for the purpose of personal formation but to liberate it for the purpose of self-expression.

The Sexual Revolution

Reflecting on Reich's thought is also helpful for understanding the nature of the sexual revolution that has now marked Western society for over half a century. To consider this—the transformation in sexual morality that has swept the West since the 1960s—as something that involves merely the expansion of the range of legitimate sexual activities and expressions is really to miss the point. For example, the sexual revolution is not simply about the legitimation of homosexuality where previously it was forbidden. Rather, it is about challenging the very nature and legitimacy of sexual codes in themselves.

One illustration of this is the fate of modesty in the modern world. These typically focused on how much skin (typically female skin) could be revealed in a public setting. How long should a skirt be? Are bikinis acceptable beach attire? These questions were matters of degree. They assumed the legitimacy of the concept of modesty and then raised the issue of the boundaries or limits of what could be considered modest.

That such questions as those preoccupied with the length of skirts seem rather quaint today is testimony to the nature and power of the sexual revolution. The sexual revolution did not redefine modesty; it overthrew it completely. Even to raise such questions as to the modesty of bikinis or skirt length today will likely elicit at best laughter and at worst some rebuke for daring to tell somebody else how to dress. In short, the very concept of modesty is now considered to be repressive, an oppressive assault upon individual authenticity.

For the sexual revolution, as for Reich, the existence of moral principles indicates that sexual needs are not being met. And in a world where sexual needs are foundational to identity, that means identities are being suppressed or denied. The game, therefore, is not to change those principles or merely loosen them. It is to abolish them in their entirety.

Of course, Reich's rhetoric is not matched by his own arguments at points. He is quite confident, for example, that a sexual relationship between an adolescent male and a prepubescent girl is illegitimate. Speaking of the boy whose sexual relationship with a girl of the same age should be encouraged, under pain of legal sanction for not doing so, he then comments,

> If the same boy of fifteen were to induce three-year-old girls into sexual games or if he tried to seduce a girl of his own age against her will, such conduct would be antisocial. It would indicate that he is neurotically inhibited in his capacity to choose a partner his own age.[11]

The question, of course, is why this should be the case? Why do age difference and the matter of consent become the only criteria of legitimate sexual activity? Are these not also "strict moral principles" of the kind that Reich has defined as "life-negating"? His own Marxist historicism, with its belief that moral principles are historically conditioned to reinforce particular forms of social oppression, would here seem to be a two-edged sword, as lethal to the new morality of sexual liberation that he affirms as to the old morality of repression that he rejects. Here we see a glimpse of the rather arbitrary, and indeed highly unstable, grounds for regulating sexual behavior that the sexual revolution involves.

The Changing Nature of Political Oppression

This specifically sexual dimension to Reich's recasting of the political question of oppression connects to a more general reformulation of left-wing political concerns. Reich makes this very clear in the preface to *The Sexual Revolution*:

> Social concepts of the nineteenth century which were defined purely in economic terms no longer fit the ideological stratifications in the cultural struggles of the twentieth century. In its simplest formulation: today's social struggles are being waged between those forces interested in the safeguarding and affirming of life and those whose interest lie in its destruction and negation.[12]

This is a critical point because it explicitly places the modern notion of the self—that of the psychologized individual—at the center of the political struggle. Whereas in the nineteenth century, the big questions were those of economic inequality, by the 1930s Reich sees them as shifting into the psychological domain. We might say that the big question is now whether society will allow people to be themselves—which in Reich's mind is the same as "give support and affirmation to individuals as they express their sexual desires in their social context." Augusto Del Noce, the Italian philosopher, describes this shift in left-wing political priorities as follows:

> It is clear that what today is called the left fights less and less in terms of class warfare, and more and more in terms of "warfare against repression," claiming that the struggle for the economic progress of the disadvantaged is included in this more general struggle, as if the two were inseparable.[13]

Reich was writing in the 1930s. Del Noce penned those words in the early 1970s. And the world we inhabit today bears more witness to the truth of this than either man could have anticipated. In the West, the struggle for freedom has become very much focused on the struggle for social recognition of a variety of sexual (and other) identities.

The term *recognition* is important here. By *recognition*, I mean not simply the commonsense notion of realizing that some claim to a particular identity exists; that, say, David claims to be gay. Rather, I mean that society does not simply tolerate David's identity while not really approving of it but actively affirms, supports, and encourages it. In other words, it is not enough to say to David that society will allow him to behave as he wishes in private without fear of prosecution. That is mere tolerance. Society must also affirm that his identity is as valid as that of anybody else, lest he feel marginalized through psychological oppression. This is a matter we will discuss further in chapter 6.

Conclusion

With Freud, we find the psychologized self we noted in Rousseau and the Romantics being given a decidedly sexual shape. Not only is the inner space of feeling now fundamental to identity; it is also defined primarily by its sexual desires. Sex is no longer a matter of behavior, of what we do; it is a matter of who we are. This helps us to understand why language such as "straight," "gay," and "bisexual" now make sense, even if one is a virgin and has never engaged in sexual activity. It is not the act but the desire, or the orientation of that desire, that defines the person. This changes everything.

Reich and those who stand in his wake make explicit the obvious implications of this shift. If a person is in some deep sense the sexual desires that they experience, then how society treats those desires is an extremely important political question. Further, the political struggle itself shifts into the psychological realm: oppression is now not simply something that involves being deprived of material prosperity or physical freedom. It is something that has a psychological component. And while Reich brings out in sharp terms the implications of this for sexual codes, for education of children, and for society's attitudes to sexual behavior, it has implications far beyond sex. We can now see that once identity is psychologized, anything that is seen to have a negative impact upon someone's psychological identity can potentially come to be seen as harmful, even as a weapon, that does serious damage. This includes those words and ideas that stand over against those identities that society chooses to sanction. This has clear implications for traditional freedoms: religion and speech.

Study Questions

1. When and how did sex become political?

2. What is the difference between tolerance and recognition?

3. What do you think defines morality for most people today?

4. In what ways does personal taste shape our morals?

The Revolt of the Masses

Introduction

The story of the modern self we have traced so far has been the story of how a number of key thinkers have thought of the self over time. I chose them because I believe them to be intellectual influences on our modern culture and, by their self-conscious reflections upon the nature of the self, they also allow us to see the implications of the changes that have taken place. But this all begs a rather obvious question: How have the thoughts and ideas of thinkers whose books and even names may be unknown to the majority of people today come to inform the intuitions of the man and woman in the street? How have we moved from the arguments of a few elite thinkers to the instincts of the masses?

That question is a variation on a perennial problem with which historians routinely wrestle: Are societies driven by ideas of philosophers and thinkers or by material factors such as economic relations or technology? Do we think the way we do because of the social conditions in which we live, or does the way we think shape those conditions? A strand of crude Marxism holds that cultural values are simply a reflection of underlying economic realities. A type of idealism holds that it is thought, especially that of the leadership class, that is the decisive factor in the way societies are organized and behave. And between these two positions are a myriad of approaches that seek to negotiate the relationship between the two.

It is not the purpose of this book to solve this problem, even if the problem were soluble in some absolute sense—something that I doubt. Yet I am aware that in laying out the intellectual genealogy of our present age, I have offered an account of what philosophers call necessary preconditions for our current situation, not sufficient preconditions. The distinction is important. A necessary precondition is something that must be true prior to something else. Thus, for apples to fall from trees, there must be some force that we call gravity pulling them down. Gravity is here a necessary precondition. But for a particular apple to fall from a particular tree at a particular time, there has to be a particular cause—say, the farmer shaking the tree or a bird pecking at the apple's stalk. In these latter cases, we have sufficient preconditions. These explain the particularities of a specific incident of an apple falling.

When I lay out the thinking of Rousseau, the Romantics, Marx, Nietzsche, Freud, and Reich, I am constructing a narrative of ideas which make the current authorization of inner feelings, and specifically the sexual and political dimension of those feelings, explicable in a general sense. But these figures were not the only influential thinkers in their day and generation. In fact, in the cases of Marx and Nietzsche, it is arguable that they were not particularly influential at all in their own day. Marx died in virtual penury, Nietzsche after a decade of insanity. And the latter's work attracted little serious interest in his own lifetime. The question of why these nineteenth-century thinkers became so influential in the subsequent century is therefore an intriguing one. For the purpose of this book, it is also somewhat important.

As noted above, I cannot solve the question of whether idealism or materialism is closer to the truth. What I can do, however, is outline a number of other factors that come into play in the twentieth century that serve to show why the revolution of the self, particularly in its sexualized form, is a plausible development. The critic might say at the end of this chapter that I have done little more than pile up yet more necessary preconditions and have not managed the decisive move to providing a sufficient precondition. I suspect I will be guilty as charged. But I would also respond that multiple necessary preconditions that work together to tilt our culture in a particular direction might well be sufficient evidence for the case I am making—as sufficient as any such case can be that also assumes human beings are free, intentional agents who have the ability to choose and, indeed, to do so in a manner that defies reduction to clean, neat, predetermined causes.

From a Fixed World to a Plastic World

One important part of the context of the changing understanding of the self is that of the correlative understanding of the world (which includes how we understand the self) that has also emerged over time. Indeed, the notion of the self with which we now intuitively operate in the West—that of something plastic that we believe we can shape in any way we wish—is arguably simply one example of a much broader view of the whole of reality.

To clarify this, it is useful to engage in a thought experiment. If I had been born in England in the fourteenth century, I would have lived in a world that I would have considered stable and fixed. Wherever I was born in the social hierarchy—peasant, noble, or king—that is where I would have remained. In all likelihood, I would have been born to a family that worked the soil as peasant farmers. My career path would thus have been determined at birth: I would grow up to be a peasant farmer. My geographical placement would have been fixed as well, as travel, let alone emigration, would have been difficult and pointless. Everything I needed would have been in the village or town where I was born. I would have had a wide extended family with whose members I was familiar. I would probably have met the girl I was to marry fairly early in life. I would have been baptized, married, and buried in the same church. And my children—as well as my children's children—would have experienced much the same. My religion would not be a choice since the Catholic church was the only religion available in my town. And my life on an annual basis would have been shaped decisively by the rhythm of the seasons: I needed to sow my crops in the spring, not the winter, and harvest them in the autumn, not the summer, praying for appropriate rain and sunshine in the interim. In short, my world would have been very fixed and very stable.

Our world is very different. Mass transportation, migration, education, social mobility, technology, science, medicine: all of these things and more have served to make the world a much more plastic place than it was in 1400. I will look at a few specifics below, but notice here the general picture: where once the world was fixed and therefore I needed to find my place within it (a place that was itself rather fixed), now its lack of fixity inclines me to think that the world can actually be shaped to my will. I was born the son of a small-town accountant and lived in

Gloucestershire as a child, attending a state grammar school; but, unlike my parents, I went to college, gained an undergraduate and a postgraduate degree, and, having worked at four previous institutions on both sides of the Atlantic, I am now a professor of humanities at a college in western Pennsylvania. My fate was not set by the circumstances of my birth; the world in which I live is one that I consider to be largely the result of my own free choices. Now, emigration might not be part of everyone's experience of life, but most people in the West today think of the world as far more flexible, even fluid, than anyone in 1400 would have thought. In 1400, the world seemed fixed, stable, and solid. Today it seems as pliable as playdough.

To put it bluntly, the modern cultural imagination sees the world as raw material to be shaped by the human will. Perhaps the most important factor in shaping this has been technology. To return to the medieval farmer: his life was utterly dependent upon the soil available in his locale and upon the rhythm of the seasons. Today, irrigation means that we can farm in the desert; glasshouses, insecticides, and fertilizers mean that the soil and the seasons lack the omnipotence they once possessed. Nature's authority has not been eliminated, but it has been significantly mitigated. The same goes for medicine. Diseases that were once death sentences can now be addressed with simple medications. Some, like polio, have even been eradicated. And geography is no longer the force that it was: with cheap transport, public and private, distances that were once measured in days or weeks can now be measured in hours.

From agriculture to medicine, from automobiles to computers, technology is not simply a means of doing perennial human activities with greater speed and efficiency. It changes the fundamental relationship of human beings to their environment and to each other. Neither the seasons of the year nor the geography of the land are as significant as they once were. Technology shifts the balance of power from nature toward human agency and the competition between agencies.

Technology also reinforces the focus on the individual, and upon individual satisfactions. Take something like music, a basic part of human societies throughout history and across the globe. In the past, music was always a live, and often a communal, activity. Somebody had to be playing music for it to be heard; and somebody had to be present in order to appreciate it. Now we can listen to whatever music we choose, whenever we want, and, perhaps most significant of all, we can do so in privacy. Music has been transformed from something with a primarily live and communal focus (live concerts notwithstanding) and has become most commonly an item of consumption for the individual. If expressive individualism has come to focus on personal satisfaction as the meaning of life, technology has served that cause well.

All of these things contribute to, and reinforce, a cultural imagination that tilts toward seeing the world simply as "stuff," the future as something we can make in whatever way we desire, and nature not so much as a fixed reality as something that is to be overcome and remade through technical mastery. If, as I argued in previous chapters, the modern person considers himself to be something he can create for himself, so he tends to extend that same notion to his relationship to the world in general. We no longer think of ourselves as subject to the world's fixed nature, or of it as having an objective authority or meaning. We are the ones with power, and we are the ones who give the world significance.

The Collapse of Traditional Authority

The rise of technology in its many forms represents one positive phenomenon that serves to authorize the individual as a master of the universe. On the negative side, one of the most important factors in the rising authority of the self and of our inner feelings, and of the idea that all reality has a plastic quality, is the collapse of traditional external sources of authority and identity. This is a vast subject, but three striking examples suffice to make the point: church, family, and nation.

In the West, the Reformation, with its fracturing of the church, is an obvious starting point for this. Where medieval Catholicism had an institutional unity, which gave credence to its claims to authority, the Reformation changed all that. After Luther, the Catholic Church had competitors. At first, nations, and then people in general, were able to choose their religion. And as countries allowed for religious freedom, then eventually churches became competitors in a religious marketplace, competing (to put it crudely) for adherents. This fundamentally transformed the dynamics of power between church authorities and congregants. Now the congregant was able to choose which church to attend, especially when the ownership of an automobile made it possible to travel to find a place of worship of one's choice.

We can add to the fragmentation of the church various other challenges to religious authority. The "cultured despisers" of religion have dominated the ways in which religion has been presented in art, literature, and now pop culture for many decades, making religious claims seem implausible and religious people seem either hypocritical, idiotic, or both. And the various recent scandals that have dogged churches have further shattered her moral authority and reinforced this popular image of venality and corruption. Traditional Christianity in particular is now commonly viewed as connected to imperialism, racism, and hatred of minorities, covering its own hypocrisy in these areas with the language of unctuously self-righteous piety.

If the last century has been brutal in its effect on institutional religious authority, a similar story can be told about the traditional family. Long-standing elite critique of the family as oppressive and tyrannical has found its counterpoint in popular culture. Movies, sitcoms, and soap operas routinely present families as dysfunctional. At the same time, legal changes have served to undermine traditional family structures. No-fault divorce has lowered the bar for the dissolution of marriage to nothing more than a sentimental feeling that the spouses would be happier apart than together. And the widespread existence of single-parent families, or of children in families blended after divorces, all serve to erode the stability and the authority of the family.

As to the notion of the nation, this too is now under severe strain. Of course, the nation-state as we know it is of relatively recent vintage, a nineteenth-century, post-Napoleonic idea. But that does not lessen its importance in shaping identity over the last 150 years. Now, however, it too faces serious difficulties. We see these on numerous fronts. Challenges to what we might call the myth of origins are all around us. Even America—a nation founded on a political creed and not on ethnicity or language or land—faces this issue now, as that national creed of freedom is challenged. Was the United States founded in 1776, with the Declaration of Independence, or in 1619 with the arrival of the first slaves? That the question is even asked speaks, at the very minimum, of a basic challenge to the traditional notion of America as a nation. And as other countries find their national narratives under pressure from radical criticism (Was Churchill a hero or a racist? Do countries such as Canada and Australia exist only because of the theft of land from, and subsequent exploitation of, indigenous peoples?), so the idea of the modern nation-state becomes increasingly problematic in the modern moral imagination.

The nation-state is also under pressure from immigration. As people move from one part of the globe to the other, the stories that sustain the nation as a unit become increasingly diluted as larger numbers of the populace do not share the national narrative in the same way that those who are native born do. In addition, information technology now allows individuals of one country to see events in another as they happen and to feel that somehow they too are involved in what is happening in faraway lands that they may never have personally visited. One of the striking things about the Trump administration was the outrage it provoked in nations with little or no real investment in America's internal domestic policies. The way in which Black Lives Matter—a quintessentially American movement rooted in a distinctively American narrative—has so easily been exported around the world is also indicative of this. In short, nation-states, and the notion of national identity that underlies them, are under great pressure.

Religious institutions, family, and nation have even in the recent past been three fundamental external anchors for identity. They provided much of the fixity, and thus stability and authority, of the early modern world. In answer to the question, "Who am I?" each could give an answer: You are Carl Trueman, a Christian who is the son of John and English by birth. Once those three lose their authority or become problematic or even sources of shame, the question of my identity needs to find other anchors. And the question is: Where can I do so? Shorn of such external markers, the turn inward gains yet more momentum.

To this we might add the observation of Yuval Levin concerning the reversal in the understanding of the purpose of institutions that characterizes our present age:

> We have moved, roughly speaking, from thinking of institutions as molds that shape people's character and habits towards seeing them as platforms that allow people to be themselves and to display themselves before a wider world.[1]

We can express this more bluntly: institutions are no longer authoritative places of formation but of performance. As with my earlier observation about the world shifting in the modern mind from a place of fixity to a place of plasticity or liquidity, so we see this shift in institutions too. And this all connects to the notion of the self articulated by the thinkers discussed earlier in this book. And when we once more add to this the matter of technology, specifically such things as Facebook, Instagram, and TikTok, we find that notion of life as public performance being further reinforced. Everybody can be an Oscar Wilde today (though generally without his wit and sophistication). And institutions have become party to this.

The Loss of Sacred Order

A second element in the question of the plasticity of reality relates to the matter of sacred order. The late Philip Rieff, sociologist at the University of Pennsylvania, argued that cultures have traditionally justified their moral orders—the set of values by which they organize themselves and regulate behavior—by appealing to a sacred order and the traditions rooted in that order. In other words, they regard their moral codes as having authority because they are grounded in something beyond this immediate world—the flow of Fate or the will of the gods or of God. For example, the law code of ancient Sparta was believed by the Spartans to have been given to the first king, Lycourgos, by the Oracle at Delphi. This meant that anyone who asked why a particular law existed would receive the answer "Because the law reflects the will of our gods as given to us by their representative, the Oracle." The same applies to societies built upon, say, the Torah, the Bible, or the Koran. Each would be able to justify its moral structure with reference to something beyond itself, to a sacred order.

In today's Western world, however, the notion of a sacred order has been largely abandoned. The fear of theocracy and the demands of the pluralism that marks our societies, in addition to the collapse of the authority of traditional religious institutions, have combined to make appeals to any kind of sacred order implausible and even unacceptable. When the Supreme Court of the United States can dismiss objections to gay marriage as motivated by nothing more than irrational bigotry, the culture's attitude to appeals to sacred order is all too clear: they are merely masks for disguising atavistic hatred. And, according to Rieff, that places us in an unprecedented and highly volatile situation: our cultures must now justify themselves purely on the basis of themselves. As with the collapse of the authority of church, nation, and family, this creates a vacuum of moral authority that is filled with the competing voices of a myriad of new identities and no objective way of adjudicating between them. And that means that society's moral order defaults to pragmatism and, put crudely, to the matter of who shouts loudest and has the most effective lobby groups.

Contraception, Pornography, and Sex

Reich may have been able to conceptualize the sexual revolution, but for it to become reality it had to become practically plausible. And technology played a vital part in that. If his notion of promiscuous, unattached sexual relations among teenagers had been realized in the 1930s, it would likely have led to chaos. Mass pregnancies of girls with no individual means of support would likely have required that thing which Reich despised—the traditional family—to step in and provide support. Only with the advent of cheap and efficient contraception could Reich's vision become a viable possibility for society.

The advent of the pill is central to this story. It allowed women to take control of their own fertility and made it very easy to sever the link between sex and pregnancy. This changed the context of sexual activity. In the nineteenth century, if a man wanted to have sex with a girl, it was a risky venture because it could easily lead to pregnancy and thus present serious social difficulties for him. Marriage in such a context was the safest way to pursue sexual activity, and to do so, a man likely had to be clean, had to have a job in order to persuade a woman that he could offer security, and ideally had to wait right up until the moment of marriage as she probably had a father and brothers who would have strong opinions about her being impregnated by someone who might then abandon his responsibilities. With the pill, the risks (financial and social) of sex were dramatically lowered. The idea of sex as a pleasant recreation without the need for long-term commitment is simply far more plausible in a world with access to the pill.

We might also add that the morality defending traditional sexual norms of marriage and monogamy, while not rendered implausible merely by the pill, becomes vulnerable to questions about its rationale once contraception is cheap, efficient, and widely available. As noted above, with the loss of the sense of sacred order, morality tends to default to a form of pragmatism, of what works and what does not. Arguments based on the authority of God's law or the idea that human beings are made in the image of God no longer carry any significant weight in a world devoid of the sacred. And in a world of easy and efficient contraception, claims such as "If you sleep around, you will get pregnant and have to raise a child by yourself" lose their potency. Traditional moral codes of sexuality have lost their authority on both fronts.

A further factor is the matter of pornography. While Hugh Hefner's *Playboy* played a signal role in helping to move titillating material into the cultural mainstream, it was the arrival of internet pornography that really transformed the situation. No longer does use of pornography carry the social stigma that it once did. It can be accessed privately, without the risk (or, at least, the perceived risk) that purchasing a magazine or entering certain establishments used to carry. And "porn stars" are now a staple of popular TV shows, the college lecture circuit, and the bookshelves at Barnes and Noble. Indeed, it speaks volumes that a baby onesie with the words "Future Porn Star" emblazoned on the front is today available as a real item of clothing.

Traditional objections to pornography tended to focus on the exploitation of those involved and on the inappropriate sexual lust it fueled in those consuming it. But it is surely interesting that pornography has significant philosophical affinities with the broader expressive individualism that characterizes modern Western culture. Indeed, it preaches a particular view of sex that correlates with the idea of the modern self. If the expressive individual sees personal satisfaction or happiness as central to the fulfilled human life, then pornography allows for the realization of that in sexual terms. It presents the sexual act as something whose significance is found simply in the pleasure of the observer or consumer. The traditional Christian idea that sex is the seal on a unique interpersonal, lifelong, exclusive relationship between one man and one woman, and therefore has meaning only in the context of that relationship, is not part of the philosophy of pornography. To use a distinction deployed by philosopher Roger Scruton, pornography is about bodies, not faces. If sex is just about my pleasure, any body will do as a partner. But in a marriage, the specific identity of the sexual partners is critical. The purpose of sex is not to have sex but to make love, to reinforce a relationship with a particular person—or, to use Scruton's terminology, with a face, not just with a body.

There is also an anthropological side to the rise of sex as important to identity. Once the authorizing of the inner psychological space had happened, it was perhaps inevitable that sex would become more and more significant. Sexual desires are among the most powerful inner feelings that most human beings experience. Further evidence for this is the way in which sex has been a primary focus of the moral codes of societies across the world and throughout the ages. This indicates how important sex, sexual desire, and the rules and mechanisms that corral and channel sexuality, are to human culture and how societies think about what it means to be human. To quote the cliché, sex sells—and sex sells because we like it, and it strikes a deep, appealing chord within us. If we are honest, Freud was touching on a significant truth: sex and sexual desires do shape who we are in fundamental ways. In short, we might perhaps say that human identity tilts in a sexual direction; and when external anchors of identity are weakened or even collapse, then the ideas of Freud, the availability of contraception, and the proliferation of easily accessible pornography can all find receptive soil in which to grow and make that tilt something obvious in the way our societies think and behave.

To this we might also add the burgeoning sector of social science that has placed sex and sexual satisfaction at the heart of human existence. Alfred Kinsey's reports, *On Sexual Behavior in the Human Male* (1948) and *On Sexual Behavior in the Human Female* (1953). purported to offer scientific accounts of human sexuality that challenged the naturalness of traditional sexual codes and presented a much more variegated account of human sexual activity. Though the findings have been subject to many challenges in the years since, they inspired similar research and raised widespread doubts about traditional thinking regarding sexuality. What is perhaps important here is that which political scientist Jacob Blakely calls "the double hermeneutic effect" of social sciences. This is the idea that "an interpretation of the world [offered by a social science] actually shapes the very interpretations that comprise it."[2] Put in simple terms, this means that the models we use to explain the world do not so much reflect the way the world is as impose a particular shape upon the world. In short, the tradition of seeing the world as driven by sex that Kinsey's reports inaugurate is responsible for the fact that we now see the world as driven by sex. We might say that we find the world to mean what we expect it to mean. And when those with authority (such as scientists) tell us what we should expect it to mean, our observations will confirm this. Kinsey and his cultural heirs—whether a sex sociologist such as Shere Hite, an entrepreneur like Hugh Hefner, the barons of the pornographic industry, or the sex therapists of myriad TV shows—tell powerful stories of how sex and sexual pleasure are the key to a happy human existence.

And that fact helps to explain why we think that sex and sexual pleasure are the key to human existence.

The Revolt of the Elites

One of the unusual hallmarks of modern Western society, in contrast to those that preceded it, is the role of the cultural elites. The historical role of such was traditionally that of the transmission of values from one generation to the next. Thus, the religious authorities passed on the faith and taught respect for the church; national leaders encouraged patriotism; and the family cultivated respect for parents and grandparents. In education, particularly in the humanities, teachers sought to draw on the perceived wisdom of the past in order to shape people to be good citizens. Each promoted a vision of the self that had obligations to others and indeed to the past. While there were inevitably changes as time went on, a basic respect for the past characterized their role.

Today, this cultural role has been transformed into its opposite. The fields of politics, art, education, and corporate business are now all marked by an aggressive negativity toward the past and its values and beliefs. The political drive on the left to overthrow traditional notions of sexual morality and human identity and that on the populist right, with its rhetoric of contempt for traditional democratic institutions, both witness to a deep commitment to tearing down the values of the past. Burn the past to the ground is the underlying mantra of political radicals on both sides.

Education—at universities and colleges but also increasingly at high schools and below—is permeated with the politics of identity and the various critical theories that see the purpose of pedagogy to be that of unmasking social inequalities in the pursuit of social justice. The underlying logic of Rousseau's theory of culture—that it is necessarily corrupting and oppressive—has found a myriad of expressions in the modern classroom as traditional social mores are decried as colonialist, sexist, imperialist, and racist. Battles over which books should be read in literature courses and which topics studied in history curricula bear eloquent witness to this. And the sex education of minors is an area of ongoing and acrimonious debate, focusing attention both on the clash between the values of the past and those of the present, and on that between parental rights and those of the state.

The world of the arts and entertainment is much the same. Movies, sitcoms, and even commercials now promote the mores of the sexual revolution and mock those who dissent from the consensus. As to music, we have come a long way from the moment in the 1960s when the Rolling Stones had to change the lyrics of the song "Let's Spend the Night Together" to "Let's Spend Some Time Together" in order to be allowed to appear on *The Ed Sullivan Show*. Songs marketed to young teenage girls now routinely contain sexually explicit lyrics far beyond anything Mick Jagger ever recorded, and often accompanied by videos that flaunt the singers' sexuality in graphic ways.

And to this mix we can add the world of corporate business. While for many years big business was identified in the West with conservative political causes—probably in large part because the concept of free enterprise stood in obvious opposition to old left thinking on socialism and economics—this has now given way to support for radical social causes. One can debate the reason for this—an inherent libertarianism in the philosophy of big tech firms such as Amazon and Facebook? A cynical attempt to capitalize on youth markets?—but one cannot deny the reality. When in 2015 the Indiana state legislature attempted to pass a Religious

Freedom Restoration Act to protect the religious consciences of business owners in light of the emerging push for LGBTQ+ rights, the backlash from big corporations was so swift, widespread, and effective that the final bill signed into law was considerably weaker in its stipulations than the original. Big business had shown that it too was committed to a market that was overthrowing the values of the past, particularly in matters of religious freedom and sexual mores. And that scenario has been repeated with matters such as transgender bathroom policies and voting reform. Big business is firmly on the side of progressivism, as the ubiquity of the LGBTQ+ rainbow flag in store windows and corporate websites during Pride Month now testifies.

In short, the role of the cultural elites today is not to maintain continuity with the past, to preserve its beliefs and practices, or perhaps to modify them to make them fit contemporary conditions but still to do so in a way that respects and stands in continuity with previous generations. Rather, it is to overthrow them in the pursuit of establishing the new values, those of expressive individuals who need to be liberated from those historical cultural chains that inhibit them from being truly themselves and society from being truly free and just.

Conclusion

As I noted at the start of this chapter, it is likely impossible to present a watertight account of why we modern men and women think intuitively about the world in the way that we do. Yet one can certainly offer an account that piles up various necessary preconditions for this and observe how these tend to tilt us in a particular direction. The collapse of traditional, external anchors of identity—perhaps most obviously those of religion, nation, and family—explains the attraction of the turn inward. The rise of technology feeds the notion that we can bend nature to our will, that the world is just so much raw, plastic material from which we can make whatever meaning or reality we choose. The loss of sacred order reinforces this subjectivism, as Nietzsche anticipated in *The Gay Science*. And the notion that sexual freedom is central to a happy human life is made a practical option by contraception and part of our cultural imagination both by the pornographic industry and by the apparently authoritative claims of social science. And then there is the role of the elites, political, educational, cultural, and business, who have all decided both to repudiate the past and to press home the pathologies of the modern, expressive, sexual self with all the power available to them. The expressive self of the sexual revolution may not be a necessary development; but all of these factors make it a most coherent and explicable one.

Study Questions

1. What effect did the advent of the birth control pill have on the sexual revolution?

2. Which traditional external anchor of identity do you feel is most significantly under attack: religion, family, or nation?

3. How has the presentation of families in pop culture and entertainment served to undermine their traditional authority?

6

Plastic People, Liquid World

Introduction

The narrative of chapters 2 to 5 is not in any sense exhaustive, but it does indicate the major contours of the modern self: the emphasis on the authority of our inner feelings; the centrality of sexual desire to this; the way in which this is now a political and not merely a personal matter; and the various cultural and technological factors that have also served to promote this way of understanding the self.

Before moving to look at some specific ways in which this modern notion of selfhood is reshaping our world, it will be useful to reflect upon a few important general concepts that provide a framework for better understanding the particular issues that face us. The first is the nature of personhood; the second is the politics of recognition; and the third is the power of imagined communities. Reflecting upon these three will help us to understand the distinctive nature of the culture in which we now find ourselves. For our culture is one marked by plastic people who believe they can make and remake themselves at will; and by a liquid world in which, to borrow a phrase from Karl Marx, all that is solid seems continually to melt into air. The coincidence of these two things—plastic people and a liquid world—is central to the issues we now face in our culture, from identity politics and LGBTQ+ rights to the growing impatience in some quarters with traditional freedoms such as those of speech and religion. But before we can look at those specifically, we need first to clarify the terms of discussion.

What Is a Person?

When we reflect upon personal identity, it quickly becomes clear that we are more than that of which we are made. What exactly do I mean by this? Well, there is a sense in which I could be defined in terms of the various chemical compounds that make up my body—water, salt, fats. That might not, of course, be sufficient to define me as this particular individual, but this could easily be rectified with attention to my genetic code. Were I to commit a crime, for example, and leave some droplets of blood or a few skin cells at the scene, a forensic scientist would be able to prove that I, and not some other character, was present when the burglary was committed.

And yet if I am asked who I am, it is very unlikely that I am going to respond by telling the inquirer my genetic code. It is true that the chemicals that constitute my body and the genetic code that provides my unique biological nature are *what* I am. But they are not *who* I am. To be a person is to be something more. It is to be someone with a particular history. To ask who I am is not to demand to know what makes me biologically distinct from other human beings but to ask about my life, about the people, places, actions, and events that have shaped my sense of identity.

We can feel a sense of this by asking ourselves what it would be like to have been born in a different time and place and to different parents. What if I had been born in France in 1770 to a family of French nobles, rather than in England in the 1960s to a family of the lower middle class? This question makes my head spin because it is really impossible to answer. Even if that version of me had the same genetic code, he would not be me in any meaningful sense of the word. I am in an important sense constituted by the social relationships that I have with other people and the ways in which they have shaped my experience of the world and my understanding of my own history.

We can press this further. We all like to assume that our identity is a monologue. After all, we feel intuitively free. Our lives are full of decisions that we have made. Some are trivial (what to eat for breakfast, for example) and some are momentous (where we study, what career we pursue, whom we marry), but they are all decisions made by us with a deep sense of freedom. Yes, there are some things we have no power over—the identity of our parents would be an obvious instance of such. But even with our family, we have significant freedom over how we relate to them as we grow up. We could choose to remain close to our parents and siblings, or we could repudiate them entirely. Is my identity therefore not in large part a matter of my own free choice?

In a sense, yes, it is. Human beings are intentional creatures. We shape our own destinies, unlike other creatures. Beavers build dams because they are instinctively disposed to do so. Cats catch mice because that is what cats do. Neither beavers nor cats reflect upon these actions, nor do they decide to do them in the sense that I might decide to paint a picture, build a wall, or go fishing. As a human being, I can act intentionally. I can conceive of the future, and I can act relative to that future in a manner that chooses to pursue one course of action instead of another. I also have scores of beliefs about myself and the world in which I live, beliefs that I can choose to change if I so wish. In short, I intuit myself as a free agent. Freedom and intentionality characterize my life. So is my identity not a matter of me deciding to be this kind of person and not that?

In fact, the situation is more complicated than this intuitive understanding of self implies. This is because human beings also act in dialogue with their surroundings. To put it very simply, we do not make these intentional decisions in a vacuum. Rather, we make them in the context of the societies we inhabit, and their wider histories in which we are placed—societies whose framework provides the means by which our actions have meaning.

To take a banal example: Think of a typical teenager. There is no person more prone to emphasize independence and freedom than a teenager wanting to assert their emerging adulthood by breaking free the constraints placed upon them by parents. Often this manifests itself in choice of clothing. Fashion is now frequently designed to be a deliberate and conscious, often iconoclastic, contrast with that which preceded it and therefore to mark off the rising generation from previous ones. On occasion, it can be very specifically intended to represent a form of positive rebellion: the arrival of blue jeans in the 1950s and of miniskirts in the 1960s are two obvious examples, but every generation has its own sartorial idioms for expressing its freedom and distinctiveness. Yet this choice of clothing, while intended as a display of individuality and independence, often leads teenagers to adopt a remarkably conformist appearance. In short, teenagers frequently all look, dress, and talk like each other.

This highlights the fact that human beings do not simply wish to be free. We also wish to belong, to be part of a group where we are accepted and affirmed. We are social creatures and thrive best in situations where we are connected to others and have a sense of communal identity. The terms of belonging to any group or community—its grammar, syntax, and vocabulary—are not things that we as individuals invent but that are constituted by the society in which we find ourselves, of which we desire to be a part, and by which we want to be recognized. The teenager who wants to express her freedom does so by wearing the uniform of the group to which she wishes to belong. She may well be rebelling against the norms set by her parents, but she is conforming to a framework established by those with whom she wishes to identify. The same is true of society as a whole. We may be intuitively free and intentional in our actions, but we also wish to belong to a group or groups that make us feel valued. This leads us to the politics of recognition.

The Politics of Recognition

As I noted in chapter 4, by the term *recognition*, I do not intend the commonsense meaning of the word whereby I might look in the mirror and recognize my own face staring back at me or pass a neighbor in the street and call out to them by name in greeting. Rather, I mean the kind of recognition that is given to us in the act of belonging to a community by having our identity as part of that community recognized.

A trivial example helps to illustrate this. Many of us remember schoolyard events from our childhood when an informal game of some team sport would be organized during a lunchbreak. Typically, two individuals would be captains and would take turns to select individuals to play on their teams. To be the first pick was usually accompanied with a feeling of pride and achievement because the captain was acknowledging that you were skillful at the game and important for a winning strategy. That is a form of recognition. In an alternative scenario, however, we can imagine being the child who is picked last. That experience is typically characterized by a feeling of dejection and failure. It always hurts to be the last pick. Using more technical vocabulary, we might say that it precipitates a feeling of alienation. In this latter case, the child has not been recognized and his value has not been affirmed.

This trivial example sets forth the kind of situation in which human beings find themselves in society where the granting or withholding of recognition is key to a sense of community and belonging. Societies as a whole have frameworks for recognition. We might call this their ethical structure: the set of cultural standards and expectations to which individuals need to conform in order to be considered full members of a particular society or community. Refusal to conform to these norms is likely to result in a refusal of full membership—a denial of full recognition—to the one who is deviant by the relevant standards.

For example, take the idea of the nation-state. To belong to the nation-state, one must act in accordance with the principles dictated by the values of patriotism. Thus, between 1939 and 1945 in Britain, giving assistance to members of the German Wehrmacht was inconsistent with being a British patriot and liable to render one subject to prosecution as a traitor. The same kind of principles apply to a family. Many of us remember misbehaving in some fashion and hearing our parents utter words such as "No member of this family behaves in that way!" Families assume certain standards of behavior, and to contravene them is to contradict one's status and invite ostracism. The church practice of excommunication, casting somebody out of the ecclesiastical community, witnesses to this as well: if you refuse to conform to the expected standards of behavior, you will face the consequences. In each case, the traitor, the delinquent child, and the heretic are denied recognition because they have acted outside of the moral framework of the community.

In sum, each society or community has its own rules of recognition that determine who belongs and who does not. We might also add that the refusal of recognition, as any last pick in a schoolyard game scenario knows, is a painful, demeaning experience. This will be important in chapter 7 for understanding why tolerance was never going to be enough for the LGBTQ+ community and why cake bakers and florists who refuse to serve gay weddings have so easily been turned into villains by the wider culture. Here, however, I want to connect the issue of recognition to my observation in chapter 5 concerning the collapse of nations, religious institutions, and the family as sources of authority and anchors of identity.

Imagined Communities

In an influential book, *Imagined Communities*, the political scientist and historian Benedict Anderson argued that the idea of the nation-state involved an imagined community.[1] Nations almost by definition involve so vast an area of geographical space, such large populations, and so many individual communities—villages, towns, cities—that it is impossible for everyone to know everyone else. This means that, for a nation to exist, its members must imagine that they hold things in common that give them a coherent identity as a body of people. The hairdresser in Cornwall must identify in some way with the docker in Tyneside for the concept of England to have any real authority. The trucker in Seattle must identify at some deep level with the restaurant owner in Florida if the idea of America is to make any sense.

What binds them together, of course, is in part a strong national narrative, something that gives them a sense of history, a sense of belonging, a sense of pride—in short, a sense of identity. In Britain, there were patriotic songs that spoke to this—"Land of Hope and Glory" for the English, "Scotland the Brave" for the Scots, and "Land of my Fathers" for the Welsh. The American national anthem and the calendar, marking those dates in the nation's history that define its identity—Thanksgiving, the Fourth of July, Veterans Day, Martin Luther King Jr. Day—all serve to press the power of the national narrative onto the population. These national narratives provided the basis for patriotism, the commitment to a national cause that motivated men to sign up for the army in the First and Second World Wars. Their identity was so wrapped up with the nation that a strike against their country was a strike against them; to risk death for that country was a comprehensible act because a threat to the nation was a threat to each and every one of them and their families. In short, even though few of them actually knew each other in their real, daily lives, they still saw themselves as all belonging to a community whose cause they saw as greater than themselves. That, we might note, is true belonging. And it is rooted in the imagination. That does not mean this sense of belonging is imaginary, in the sense of not being true or not really existing. But it does mean that it is rooted in a way of thinking and not in the fact of personal acquaintance with every other member of the community.

Yet this is where our current situation becomes rather complicated. What happens when the narratives that provide us with our traditional identities lose their authority and become highly contested? When the ways in which we belong start to fall apart? That is another way of describing the phenomenon we noted in chapter 5 with specific reference to the collapsing authority of nation, religion, and family. If the perennial need to belong persists, where do human beings find that "belonging" in a world where the traditional forms of such belonging are no longer plausible or, to use Anderson's terminology, where traditional communities can no longer be imagined as they once were?

To answer this, it is first useful to note once again that technology plays a key role here. If technology in the form of the pill helped to undermine traditional sexual codes, then in the form of the internet it helps to weaken the traditional narratives of our imagined communities and offers others to replace them. Indeed, information technology now means that there is a multitude of competing narratives and, consequently, so many different ways of imagining communities. If the imagined community of the nation depended upon an agreed national story and means by which that national story could be promoted and maintained, then that assumed there were coherent means of telling that story. In short, a unified community assumed limited information that allowed for a single dominant narrative to give coherence to the whole.

This is not to argue for the need for censorship of information such as we now see in China. That too has a distorting impact on a people's sense of identity. It is simply to note that the explosion of information facilitated by technology is having a profound effect on how we in the West think of ourselves. For example, when I was a child in Britain, there were only three television channels. That meant that the national news was presented by a tiny handful of programs. New movies had to be watched at the cinema because it was years before they would be licensed for the television. There were perhaps fewer than ten national newspapers, of which only about half offered serious news analysis. Knowledge of the rest of the world was mediated by newsprint, photographs, and the occasional piece of video footage. Even America seemed a long way away. In short, the national narrative was strong because the dominant media voices were few and, while not all in total agreement, operating within reasonably narrow narrative boundaries. And the alternatives were weak or nonexistent. Yes, the *Morning Star* offered a Marxist commentary on Britain, but it was read by almost nobody and carried no serious weight at mainstream institutions. It was certainly very hard to be in a significant "imagined community" with people on the other side of the world. This was one reason why, in the late nineteenth and early twentieth centuries, Marxist revolutionaries were constantly frustrated that class identity proved weaker than national, religious, and familial identities. There was no real means by which to create an imagined community that united workers across the globe with stronger ties than the dominant national narratives.

Today, all that has changed. National narratives are not the means for social unity but have instead become battle zones, and it is very hard to be part of an imagined community when the nature of what is to be imagined is itself a primary source of division. But not only are the narratives of nations being contested; they are facing challenges from other narratives and other ways of being imagined communities. A moment's reflection indicates this: the language of community is now routinely applied to categories that have little or nothing to do with nation or religion or family. There is the black community, the LGBTQ+ community, the Asian community, the disabled community, even the BDSM (bondage, discipline, dominance and submission, sadomasochism) community. The use of the word *community* for these various groups indicates both the collapse of traditional notions of belonging and the rise of a vast and growing number of alternative ways of human beings imagining their relationship to those around them. When identity is grounded in psychology and the internet allows for the indulgence of any and all means of thinking about that identity, the concept of community lacks any real solidity. People can now pick and choose their communities, and that means that they can pick and choose their identities.

One intriguing and instructive example is that provided by the emergence of the Islamic State, or ISIS. At numerous points during the years when it dominated headlines in the West, I frequently heard some version of the following phrase used with regard to young, affluent Westerners who had chosen to identify with its cause: "He pledged allegiance to ISIS online." There are many interesting aspects to such a statement: What does it mean to "pledge allegiance online"? How has the online world come to hold such a grip on imaginations that such an act makes sense to some individuals? These questions rest upon the most obvious fact that the statement reveals: the various individuals who did this clearly "imagined" that the ISIS community—even when exclusively mediated to them via its online presence on websites and blogs—was a more powerful source of belonging and identity than their families or the nations to which their passports indicated they belonged. Only in a world where the old forms of belonging have been dramatically weakened and new forms of community have gained imaginative traction can pledging allegiance online to ISIS come to make any sense.

The role of media and information technology in this has an importance that can scarcely be exaggerated. Geography is far less significant now than under the old imagined community of the nation-state. As Anderson's notion of an imagined community makes clear, geography was not itself the central factor even there because nations presupposed a sense of common identity that was not built on personal proximity or acquaintance. Given the fact that nations have borders, it was necessary that, for example, Americans in Texas live closer to Mexico than to Maine and yet still feel greater affinity for, and identity with, the inhabitants of Portland than those of Guadalajara. I grew up forty miles from Wales and hundreds of miles from Newcastle. But like the natives of Newcastle, I consider myself English. Even so, geography was still somewhat significant as locating key institutions, defining national territory, and providing a physical context for the national narrative. None of that applies in the age of the internet.

Indeed, time and space are both transformed by the internet. The web can provide an immediacy of both, which was unknown to earlier generations because it was simply impossible. As it does so, it then enables, even encourages, people to reimagine the communities to which they belong. As the worldwide protests of the summer of 2020 indicate, a police action in the United States can seem more real and immediate to people around the world than events in a neighboring town. When British people were marching to protest the death of George Floyd, I was struck by the lack of similar protests in Britain concerning the ongoing struggle for human rights in Hong Kong. Hong Kong has a much closer historical connection to the British national narrative than does Minneapolis, and, while it may be farther away, in the age of jet air travel, that is hardly a significant factor—a matter of just a few hours' difference. Even so, events in this midwestern American city seemed far more immediate and real to many British people, far more relevant to the emerging "imagined community" of anti-racists and social justice activists than events in a place that was a British colony until as recently as 1997. The national narrative has disappeared and a new narrative, that of social justice and anti-racism, has emerged to take its place.

Furthermore, it is not simply the immediacy of the internet but also the sheer volume and variety of information it offers that has transformed how we think about the world. The three British TV channels of my youth have been replaced with hundreds of the same. Websites offer a seemingly infinite amount of information, readily available at the click of a mouse. The ability for a single narrative, or a small handful of narratives, to dominate the airwaves is long past. In this sense, we might argue that there is one unifying narrative that lies behind the diversity of competing narratives on offer. It is that of the power of the individual to choose his or her identity. No longer are we presented with powerful, fixed narratives such as that of nation, family, or even bodily sex. Now we are free to choose the narrative to which we wish to belong, the imagined community that will provide us with our identity and purpose. We can focus on those narratives that make us feel good and that confirm our chosen view of the world and ignore those that present challenges to this. If the Reformation made religion a choice and represented a key move in placing the individual at the center of things, the internet has extrapolated that to vast swaths of life. We can now choose our narratives and our communities more easily than previous generations chose clothes and shoes.

Recognition and Narrative

When we connect the two parts of this chapter, the issue of recognition and the emergence of new imagined communities, the current conflicts that are causing such tensions within Western democracies start to make sense. Our societies are formally organized along the lines of the old community of the nation-state. We have institutions and calendars that reflect the imagined community of the nation. We still grant one vote to each person in California and one to each person in Arkansas on the grounds that we share a common cause, that of the United States as a nation. Yet so many members of that society made up of American citizens now find that the narratives that most strongly shape their identities are not those of the nation-state but rather those of race, ethnicity, gender, sexuality, etc. They can chat to friends across the globe online. They can see political events unfolding as they happen in far-off countries and feel an empathy for the people they immediately affect. They can feel an affinity for those who share the same skin color or sexual orientation in other countries, an affinity they may not feel for the neighbor living next door with whom they do not share such things. That is a situation in which conflict is bound to occur. Indeed, this explains why the social justice narrative despises our established institutions—they see them as systemically racist because they are constructed around a different understanding of identity. And it also explains why both time (Should we celebrate Columbus Day or Juneteenth?) and space (Which names are appropriate for buildings? Whose statues should be allowed to stand where?) are arenas of this conflict: the conquest of time and space by the new narratives is critical to them gaining hold of the popular imagination.

In the past, civil society was possible because, whatever the differences that existed between citizens, there was a deeper narrative, a deeper sense of identity and community, that all shared and that served to relativize such. Therefore, when an election was won by one party, adherents of the other party respected the results because something deeper than party politics—the nation itself—was strong enough to provide a sense of underlying unity. As the elections of Donald Trump in 2016 and Joseph Biden in 2020 have demonstrated, this is no longer the case. Modern American society is fragmenting because the imagined communities to which people choose to belong lack any shared narrative. Therefore, the terms of recognition that one group wishes to see American society adopt are often antithetical to those of others. And this leads to further conflict because the very existence of alternative narratives is a threat to a given community's identity.

The importance of this will become clear when we look at the challenges that the rise of the LGBTQ+ movement poses to traditional freedoms, such as those of speech and religion. Such things were once considered basic essentials to a free society. Now they are coming to be seen not merely as unimportant social luxuries but as antithetical to a truly just and free society.

Conclusion

All of the above points to the fact that we now live at a time when the very issue of identity is an unstable, volatile, highly contentious, and even unprecedented matter. Now, it is not unusual for commentators on contemporary events, whether professional critics or amateur pundits, to make hyperbolic claims about "crises" and "living in unprecedented times." That is usually the moment at which the trained but annoying historian steps forward with a condescending smile and declares that, no, actually there is a precedent—maybe fourteenth-century Florence or sixteenth-century Spain or Germany between the wars—and that, yes, we have seen all this before. There is often much truth to such responses, as we all have a tendency to think of our own era and our own problems as unprecedented and uniquely challenging. We need to be reminded that this is not typically the case. I would argue, however, that the coincidence of two things makes our current moment in time a singularly challenging and potentially sinister one.

These two things are the plastic conception of human identity to which expressive individualism tilts; and the liquefaction of the world around us with regard to the traditional frameworks (national, religious, familial, geographical, even physiological) by which human beings have previously defined themselves. That places us in a situation without obvious historical parallel. In the past—at least the past of the last few hundred years in the West—there has been sufficient cultural and institutional continuity over time to offer some stable framework for each person to find their identity in something that offered stability. Again, to repeat the mantra: nation, church, and family were perhaps the three most obvious. But even as these became increasingly tenuous in the late twentieth century, our bodies still offered some minimal level of continuity and stability. The person born with a male body did not have to decide his gender. It was a given, over which he had no authority. The mother who gave birth to a daughter did not wake up twenty years later to find that her daughter no longer existed but was now a son.

Today, the self is entirely plastic, and the external world—right down to our bodies—is liquid, something that offers no firm ground upon which to build an identity. That no doubt helps to explain, for example, the catastrophic levels of depression and anxiety in the West which, on the whole, enjoys greater material prosperity and security than has been typical throughout human history. Yes, we are wealthier and healthier than our ancestors in the sixteenth and even the mid-twentieth centuries. But we do not know who we are anymore. As terrifying as that is to contemplate, it seems undeniable. Jean-Paul Sartre's comment that man is condemned to be free[2] seems to capture something of our moment in time, for freedom without belonging is a grim burden to bear.

This also helps to explain the power of newly emerging identities such as those offered by the LGBTQ+ movement. In a world where old identities are implausible and where people still wish to belong, the most powerful narratives and the strongest communities can offer a sense of belonging and security that all human beings crave. As we will note in the next chapter, the dominant narratives pushed by the cultural elites press us to think of human selfhood not simply in terms of expressive individualism but specifically in terms of sexual identity. They also encourage us to see sexual fulfillment as a core component of a happy and fulfilled life. They shape our sentiments to see victimhood and marginalization not simply as evils to be overcome but also as granting the victimized and the marginal a moral status that makes their various causes something that it is nearly impossible to oppose.

Human selves exist in dialogue with the terms of recognition set by the wider world. When that world is liquid, those terms are set by the loudest voices and the most dominant narratives. It is to those voices and narratives as found in the LGBTQ+ movement that we now turn in chapter 7.

Study Questions

1. Where have you seen yourself acting as an expressive individual in your life?

2. What shared narrative or culture do you try to cultivate in your family?

3. What community do you find yourself putting your identity in?

4. How far are you willing to go to defend your values in today's society?

5. In what ways are our current times unprecedented? In what ways are they not?

6. In what ways has the expansion of the internet altered modern communities?

7

The Sexual Revolution
of the LGBTQ+

Introduction

The letters LGBTQ+ loom large in the cultural and political imagination of our day. The coalition of lesbian, gay, bisexual, trans and queer people is without a doubt the greatest political success story of the last half century. In the 1960s, homosexuality was still illegal in many Western countries. Even Barack Obama did not dare to support gay marriage unequivocally until 2012. Yet today, even to voice dissent from trans ideology is likely to earn one a ferocious social media beating and exclusion from polite liberal society. The speed, depth, and comprehensive scope of the LGBTQ+'s triumphant cultural conquest is impressive.

Yet familiarity with the coalition can easily blind observers to its confected and volatile nature. It is not a movement bound together by a set of intrinsic commonalities shared by its constituent groups, as, say the Republican or Democratic Party are. Rather it is a marriage of convenience, created by uniquely particular circumstances. Exploring this point is helpful because it not only helps us to understand the nature of the sexual revolution that we are witnessing today; it also helps us see what exactly is at stake in all this in terms of where the revolution itself might be heading and how this will reshape public attitudes toward traditional freedoms, such as those of speech and religion (the latter two topics will be addressed in chapter 8).

LGBTQ+: A Marriage of Convenience

The first thing to note about the LGBTQ+ is that its different constituent members are actually divided over the very thing upon which an outsider might assume they are agreed: the nature and status of sex.

Consider first the L and the G. Until the early 1980s, lesbians and gay men did not operate as a united coalition. Lesbians saw gay men as enjoying male privilege. For example, a gay man in the workplace was typically not under any pressure to make himself attractive to a female boss in order to improve his professional prospects. A lesbian woman, however, might well find that she was required to play a distinctly feminine, even sexually attractive, role in a heterosexual context for career success. In short, gay men were still men and enjoyed the benefits of living in a society that gave an advantageous position to their sex. There were also differences in attitudes toward sexual activity itself. Gay men were more focused on genital sex and on orgasms; lesbians toward affection and companionship.

So what brought the L and the G together? Put simply: the AIDS crisis of the 1980s. AIDS had a disproportionate and devastating impact on gay men and transformed their image overnight from that of privileged middle-class males engaged in self-indulgence to that of tragic victims of a deadly and (at that point) uncontrollable disease that was closely connected to their sexual identity. Therefore, in the early 1980s, an interesting and public coalition of the L and the G emerged, focused on presenting a united front in the campaign for AIDS research, sex education, and the mainstream acceptance of gay and lesbian people by the wider community.

Three things are noteworthy here. First, the coalition arose out of a shared sense of victimhood. As lesbians saw themselves as victims of a heteronormative, patriarchal society, so they now saw gay men as victims of the same. This is, in part, a function of the broader culture of expressive individualism that tilts toward seeing as virtuous victims those unable to express outwardly that which they feel inwardly. We see here a good example of that politicization of the sexual self noted in chapter 4.

Second, both lesbians and gays (and bisexuals) assume the importance of biological sex differences. Lesbians are biological women who are sexually attracted to biological women. Gay men are biological men who are sexually attracted to biological men. Bisexuals are those who acknowledge their own biological identity as well as their sexual attraction to others of either biological identity.

Third—standing in significant tension with the second point—in allying themselves with gay men, lesbians set aside the importance of biology (with its significance for how different sexes experience the world and relate to patriarchal society and to sexual acts themselves) in order to present a common front against a common enemy: heteronormative society. In retrospect, this was a critical move because it ultimately paved the way for the addition of the T and the Q to the alliance on the basis that "the enemy of my enemy is my friend."

Trans Ideology

The origins of trans ideology arguably go back to the nineteenth century. In *The Communist Manifesto*, Marx and Engels noted that as production came to be increasingly automated, and as raw physical strength therefore became less significant in the workplace, the difference between men and women would shrink. Of course, they were not envisaging a world where a Caitlyn Jenner would be possible, but the link to technology is important. We might also note that Nietzsche's antimetaphysical philosophy, with its stress on how we ourselves have a godlike power to create truth, also lends itself to the repudiation of stable categories such as male and female. Both Marx and Nietzsche proved important to the rise of gender theory. In the context of this book's narrative, we might also add that the psychologizing of the self that we have described also opens possibilities for trans ideology. This essentially grants the givenness of the physical body less authority than the mind in determining identity. Indeed, the body is an instrument or the raw material for realizing or expressing identity as determined by the will.

Of more immediate significance to our current situation, however, is the thought of Simone de Beauvoir, the French philosopher whose 1949 book, *The Second Sex*, is a foundational text for modern feminist theory. She opens the second part of that work with a dramatic and far-reaching statement:

One is not born, but rather becomes, woman. No biological, psychic, or economic destiny defines the figure that the human female takes on in society; it is civilization as a whole that elaborates this intermediary product between the male and the eunuch that is called feminine.[1]

This captures in a remarkably concise form the fundamental convictions that underlie the modern trans movement. De Beauvoir makes a distinction between biology and what we now call gender. The whole idea of what it is to be a woman is a social construct, something that is not intrinsic to the female body. To use the language of a later gender theorist, Judith Butler, gender is a performance, a set of behaviors that society has come to expect from those who possess a certain kind of body. In so doing, a separation is made between sex (biologically determined) and gender (socially constructed), such that the latter floats free of any biological determination and can be made and remade at will. One is born biologically female; one becomes a woman by learning the performances required by society.

It is true that this notion contains elements of truth. Anyone who has experience of different cultures knows that the roles of men and women vary across the globe. The American ideal of masculinity is different from that which one finds in England or in South Korea. And the same goes for women. A woman in Cairo will conform to a set of cultural expectations different from those in Manhattan or Tokyo. It is therefore a relatively easy task to point out that such things as masculinity or femininity contain a large element of social construction whereby males and females internalize the behavioral expectations of the wider host culture.

To move from this rather obvious reality to the notion that sex and gender are separable and that the latter is simply a performance is a dramatic metaphysical leap, the plausibility of which depends upon a number of other prior factors. First, inner psychology must have been granted ultimate authority in human identity. Second, technology needs to have rendered the possibility of changing gender to be something that is technically plausible. Finally, the idea needed a powerful lobby group and an attractive media presence in order to help normalize the idea. The former came from its engrafting into the LGB movement; the latter in the person of Bruce, now Caitlyn, Jenner.

The narrative of this book has traced the psychologizing of identity from Rousseau onward. Technology has played its role in facilitating the trans moment on two fronts: it has generally encouraged people to view nature as mere raw material that can be changed by acts of human will; and it has allowed for bodily and hormonal manipulation so as to create the idea that gender can be altered.

The Problem of the T

The addition of the T to LGB is in a very real sense incoherent. As we noted earlier, lesbians, gay men, and bisexuals all assume the sex binary of male and female as grounded in basic biology. That point is denied by trans ideology, affirming as it does the separability of biological sex from gender. Queer ideology is similar, denying as it does the stability of the traditional categories of male and female in favor of a fluid and ever-changing range of multiple sexual identities.

Nothing reveals the problem more dramatically than personal testimony. Take, for example, the following words of a lesbian living with a partner who transitioned from female to male:

When my partner began his gender transition my lesbian identity had been central to my life and my sense of self for well over a decade, and I didn't know what his transition made me. Some people told me I was "obviously" still a lesbian, but it was just as obvious to others that I was now straight, or bisexual. It wasn't obvious to me at all, and I struggled with it for a long time.

Now I've been the partner of a trans man for as long as I was a lesbian, and I've gotten comfortable just not having a name for what I think I am. I think of myself as part of the family of queers and trans people.[2]

This woman's situation is a painful example of the confusion that fluid gender identities and trans ideology leave in their wake. When her female partner transitions to being a trans male, she still feels that she is a lesbian, sexually attracted to other women. But for her to assert this is to deny her partner's claim to be a man. However, if she affirms her partner's maleness, she must deny her own identity as a lesbian. In the end, she settles for being queer, a conveniently fluid and rather vague term that avoids the problems created by trying to think in binary terms about transgenderism.

Not all homosexuals are willing to be as accommodating as this woman. Andrew Sullivan, a gay man and an exceptionally sharp-witted and insightful journalist, made the following comment in *New York Magazine* in February 2019:

It is not transphobic for a gay man not to be attracted to a trans man. It is close to definitional. The core of the traditional gay claim is that there is indeed a very big difference between male and female, that the difference matters, and without it, homo-sexuality would make no sense at all. If it's all a free and fluid nonbinary choice of gender and sexual partners, a choice to have sex exclusively with the same sex would not be an expression of our identity, but a form of sexist bigotry, would it not?

Sullivan is far from a lone voice in this. In February 2021, Bryan Quinn, who is co-owner of Camp Boomerang RV Park and

Campground in Orleans, Michigan, found himself at the center of a storm. The campground is for gay men, and Quinn posted on Facebook that he would not be welcoming biological females onto the site, no matter how they identified in terms of gender. In short, trans men who were sexually attracted to men (biological and trans) were not welcome. This post earned him a storm of criticism for his transphobic policies. Other gay men have faced similar criticism for saying that, as gay, they do not find trans men to be sexually attractive. The destabilization of gender categories that trans ideology and queer theory demand stands in opposition to any category built upon the biological sex binary—straight, gay, or lesbian. In short, anyone who believes that the sex binary is important is vulnerable to accusations of transphobia.

Trans Ideology and Feminism

The difficulty of relating the T to the LGB finds a parallel in the response of feminists to the trans movement. Feminism is now bitterly divided between those who affirm trans women as true women and those who repudiate such, seeing them as men who are trying to deny the male privilege that has been their invisible birthright and steal false identifications with female victimhood. The latter have been dubbed TERFs or "trans-exclusionary radical feminists," a pejorative term that is intended to marginalize those who object to the increasingly dominant orthodoxy regarding sex and gender.

Two leading feminist thinkers now decried as TERFs are Janice Raymond and Germaine Greer. Neither woman could be accused of arguing that women's roles in society are so tightly tied to biology that the distinction between sex and gender is meaningless, but neither allows for them to be sharply separated either. In the words of Raymond,

Affirming that transsexual surgery cannot change the basic biology of chromosomal sex is not to say that chromosomal sex defines gender. But in some very real senses, female biology shapes female history—a history that men don't have because of their sex—including the history of menstruation, the history of pregnancy or the capacity to become pregnant, the history of childbirth and abortion, the history of certain bodily cycles and life changes, and the history of female subordination in a male-dominant society. Note that I keep saying history. To deny that female history is, in part, based on female biology is like denying that important aspects of Black history are based on skin color. As with biological skin color, female biology doesn't confer an essential femininity; rather it confers a historical reality about what it means to be born with XX chromosomes.[3]

What Raymond is saying is that sex and gender are not the same thing. The roles played by women throughout history and across cultures have varied. But biology is still a vital part of being a woman because it shapes how women experience the world. Menstruation, for example, is a distinctly female experience that has both economic and physical consequences for women, from which men are exempt by virtue of the biological constitution of their bodies. Pregnancy too shapes life. In each of these areas, biology is integral to being a woman. Bruce Jenner can undergo surgery and hormone treatment and change names to Caitlyn. But Caitlyn can never menstruate or bear a child.

Now, some may object at this point that not all women menstruate or conceive. Are they still to be considered women, then? That is a good question that merits a response. Of course, menstruation and conception are just two of the most obvious examples of how biology shapes a woman's experience of the world of her self. That a particular woman does not menstruate does not mean that her XX chromosomes have no significance for her experience of selfhood and her relationship to the world. Indeed, the denial that a woman's physical constitution is significant for who she is is rather like denying that the color of an African American woman's skin is relevant to her identity and relationship to her self and the world.

This should alert us to the logic of the argument upon which trans ideology depends: because it assumes that the body is not of primary relevance to gender identity, it consequently excludes bodily considerations from the definition of what it means to be a man or a woman. But notice: This is a circular argument. Its conclusion is already contained in its premise. This became clear in the storm of protest surrounding J. K. Rowling's comment that there must surely be a word for people who menstruate. Apparently, she was a bigot and a transphobe for daring to offer a narrative of womanhood that involved biology. Trans ideology really rests upon a psychological definition of what it means to be a woman. And such a definition, detached from anything connected to female biology, is itself a rather nebulous and fluid concept.

Germaine Greer made this point with characteristic pungency in 2015 on the *Victoria Derbyshire* show: "I've asked my doctor to give me long ears and liver spots and I'm going to wear a brown coat but that won't turn me into a ******* cocker spaniel."[4] Physical and chemical gerrymandering of the male body does not make it female. One can remove genitalia and inject oneself with female hormones, but every cell of the female body has two X chromosomes.

Greer also offers a cultural critique of trans ideology, seeing it as in a very real sense resting upon the idea that gender can be learned.

> The transsexual is identified as such solely on his/her own script, which can be as learned as any sex-typed behavior and as editorialized as autobiographies usually are.[5]

The implication of what Greer is saying here is that men who transition to being women are simply playing the roles that they, as men, think women should. Anyone who has seen the *Vanity Fair* cover picture of Caitlyn Jenner feels the force of what Greer is saying here: a scantily clad Jenner poses provocatively in just the way that a man would expect a cover girl to do.

What the response to Greer and other traditional feminists has shown is that feminism is deeply divided over trans ideology in the same way that many lesbians and gay men are: taking seriously the sex binary inevitably places one at odds with the trans movement. And it is against this background that society is witnessing a significant shift in the way in which laws relative to such matters are being framed. The conceptual language is now shifting from fixed identities rooted in the sex binary toward more psychological and therefore plastic terms: sexual orientation and gender identity. And it is as these ideas have become embodied in law that the implications of the LGBTQ+ movement become clear and unavoidable.

Sexual Orientation and Gender Identity:
The Yogyakarta Principles

Around the world, governments are framing SOGI (Sexual Orientation and Gender Identity) laws in relation to *The Yogyakarta*

Principles, named after the Indonesian city where they were formulated in 2006. This is a foundational text in connecting LGBTQ+ rights to the concept of human rights in general. Neither of the groups that formulated the original principles, the International Commission of Jurists and the International Service for Human Rights, has official governmental status. But numerous countries around the world have adopted the principles of Yogyakarta, such that it is fair to say that wherever sexual orientation or gender identity enjoys legal protections, there one can discern their underlying influence. *The Yogyakarta Principles* brilliantly summarize the political implications of the LGBTQ+ movement and will also no doubt continue to influence political and legal attitudes toward the same. From the opening paragraph, the *Principles'* underlying convictions are clear:

> All human beings are born free and equal in dignity and rights.
> All human rights are universal, interdependent, indivisible and
> interrelated. Sexual orientation and gender identity are integral
> to every person's dignity and humanity and must not be the basis
> for discrimination or abuse.[6]

The text then goes on to deplore violence against individuals who deviate from heterosexual norms and points an accusing finger (in principle 6) at governments that police sexuality and thereby encourage and promote cultures where gender-based violence and inequality are rife. This is emblematic of the logic of sex and oppression that we noted earlier in the thought of Wilhelm Reich and his followers. It is the logic of the sexual revolution.

It is not a surprise, therefore, to find that *The Yogyakarta Principles* assume as basic a sexualized form of expressive individualism as a normative definition of what it means to be truly human. The preamble states this as follows:

> Understanding "sexual orientation" to refer to each person's capacity for profound emotional, affectional and sexual attraction to, and intimate and sexual relations with, individuals of a different gender or the same gender or more than one gender;
>
> Understanding "gender identity" to refer to each person's deeply felt internal and individual experience of gender, which may or may not correspond with the sex assigned at birth, including the personal sense of the body (which may involve, if freely chosen, modification of bodily appearance or function by medical, surgical or other means) and other expressions of gender, including dress, speech and mannerisms.[7]

Notice three things here. First, the idea of sexual orientation really has no content. It is simply defined by subjective desire. It would appear that sexual attraction to anything—a woman, a frog, or a cardboard box—could qualify. The range of sexual identities is thus as vast as the potential objects of sexual desire.

Second, gender is separated from biological sex, and psychology trumps biology. The language is that of inner feelings, individual experience, and personal sense. The person's own feelings are given such authority that it is hard to see how any person might challenge an individual's view of their own identity without being immediately liable to accusations of oppression or worse.

Third, and following from this, sex is "assigned" at birth and is entirely separable from gender. In short, any judgment made by the doctor, the midwife, or the parents regarding the gender of the child based on physical sex is to be regarded as entirely provisional and indeed a potential alien imposition upon the child's real identity. While *The Yogyakarta Principles* do not go this far, some trans activists have used this logic to call for all children to be given puberty blockers until they are old enough to select their own gender.

Where these radically subjective identities become problematic is in the rights that *The Yogyakarta Principles* attaches to them. Principle 3 states the following:

> Everyone has the right to recognition everywhere as a person before the law. Persons of diverse sexual orientations and gender identities shall enjoy legal capacity in all aspects of life. Each person's self-defined sexual orientation and gender identity is integral to their personality and is one of the most basic aspects of self-determination, dignity and freedom.[8]

In plain terms, this calls for societies to recognize—that is, affirm, support, and protect—whatever subjective sexual identity any individual cares to affirm for themselves. How workable is this? Well, given the plasticity of sexual and gender identities rooted in subjective desires and feelings, it would seem to demand laws that are equally plastic. In theory, any sexual or gender identity one chooses or "feels" is to be protected. In practice, of course, this infinite plasticity is not a viable option, and the range of sexual and gender identities to be protected is going to be that shaped by the dispositions of cultural taste. The trans man or the lesbian enjoys protection; the pedophile (as yet) does not.

Perhaps the most fascinating of *The Yogyakarta Principles*, however, is principle 24, "The Right to Found a Family":

Everyone has the right to found a family, regardless of sexual orientation or gender identity. Families exist in diverse forms. No family may be subjected to discrimination on the basis of the sexual orientation or gender identity of any of its members.[9]

Here a number of factors come together. First, the whole notion of a "right" to found a family is interesting. No rationale for this right is given, but it seems safe to assume that the authors regard having a family as a key step in normalizing nonheterosexual sexual identities. To claim that having a family is a right is therefore to turn the family into a therapeutic phenomenon, something that exists primarily to make the parents feel good.

Second, the fact that men and women need each other to make babies is a fact of nature; and while the definition of family has changed over time, at its core it has always followed along tracks set by the biological sex differences of males and females. That may be a source of frustration to some, but it is a given. This is no longer the case, of course. What this principle assumes is the power of technology to overcome the natural limitations of human procreation and thereby turn the family into another institution that can be redefined to meet the therapeutic needs of the moment. The authors go on to assert that states will take all necessary measures to ensure access to adoption and "assisted procreation." What nature has declared impossible—that two men or two women might conceive a child together—technology has made possible; and what technology has made a possibility, the sexual revolution has made an imperative.

Third, we see again the logical sleight of hand that we noted with regard to trans ideology. The principle asserts that family has existed in diverse forms. That is true. Families in peasant societies, for example, are more extensive than in late modern urban environments. But as we just noted, that diversity has always been limited because of its deep connections to biology and to a basic binary distinction between male and female. To use the moderate diversity of family structures to justify naming any favored social arrangement as a "family" is to eviscerate the term of any meaningful content. This move parallels that which uses the diversity of what femininity and masculinity mean across different cultures in order to deny any significance to biological sex at all. An aspect of the truth is made into the whole truth. The result is an unassailable ideological position that presupposes that any evidence that might count against it is by definition inadmissible.

Trans Ideology Cannot Be Avoided

The trans issue has become the most pressing and intrusive aspect of the LGBTQ+ transformation of society. While gay marriage has created problems for Christian florists and cake bakers, it is arguable that most of us have not found it to impinge uncomfortably upon our lives in any obvious way. Trans ideology, however, is different. This is because so much of traditional society has been shaped by the assumed reality of the gender binary. From school bathroom facilities to sports to prisons to hospital wards and beyond, the basic distinction between male and female is all-pervasive. It shapes notions of privacy and safety. It has historically informed ideas of good manners and decorum, of modesty and public behavior. But when the binary comes to be seen as a mere social construction designed for the purpose of oppression, everything must change. And such change will be impossible for anyone to avoid or ignore precisely because it has such serious implications for public spaces and even for the relationships of parents, children, and the state.

In a significant Supreme Court case in 2020, *Bostock v. Clayton County*, the Court decided by a 6–3 majority that Title VII of the 1964 Civil Rights Act applied to trans individuals.[10] Title VII was originally intended to protect people (i.e., women) in the workplace from discrimination on the basis of sex. By applying Title VII to trans individuals, the Supreme Court basically accepted the detachment of gender from biological sex and granted legal status to the inner psychological convictions of those who believe themselves to be men trapped in the bodies of women or women trapped in the bodies of men. Trans ideology was thus confirmed as the law of the land when it came to matters of employment.

The author of the majority decision, Justice Neil Gorsuch, was careful to stress that this ruling was narrowly focused upon the workplace and not to be seen as having immediate relevance beyond that. But, of course, once trans ideology has legal status in one area, it is hard—even perhaps unreasonable—to keep it confined there. Within hours of his inauguration as president, Joe Biden signed into law an executive order, "Preventing and Combating Discrimination on the Basis of Gender Identity or Sexual Orientation."[11] Among other things, this order required public schools to open women's restrooms and changing rooms to biological men identifying as women. Women's sports too must be opened to biological men. In short, it took the underlying philosophy of Justice Gorsuch and applied it to the area of education, citing Title VII as it did so.

What this means is that trans ideology now has a grip on the law in such a way that it is going to be impossible to avoid. If you employ people, if you work with people, if your children go to the public schools, you are going to find the trans question pressing upon you. It is no longer sufficient to plead individual moral scruples with regard to these things, any more than that is deemed acceptable in matters of racial segregation. Trans rights are now civil rights, and those with principled objections have no obvious recourse by which they might protect themselves. Carried through consistently, women's sports will soon be a thing of the past, given the typical disparity of strength between male and female athletes. That will have an impact on many young women who depend upon athletic scholarships to fund their education. More tragically, young girls and boys at school now find that the one place they might have expected society to work hard to grant them privacy and protection—school restrooms—are the very places where society has not simply abdicated its responsibility but has actually created a legal culture opposed to such. The same applies to women's prisons.

Trans ideology increasingly shapes corporate policies too. The banning of Ryan T. Anderson's calm, thoughtful, and well-researched book, *When Harry Became Sally*, by Amazon in February 2021 was an interesting move. Mao, Hitler, and Stalin remained authors in good standing. The company sent out numerous emails in that very month, encouraging customers to purchase *Technological Slavery* by Theodore Kaczynski. Kaczynski is better known as the Unabomber, the United States' most infamous home-grown terrorist. This work (and his earlier *Manifesto*) are still available via Amazon. Yet even in the worst-case scenario, Anderson's book is unlikely to cause a world war, lead to millions of deaths by famine, or inspire a domestic bombing campaign. Somehow, Anderson had committed a more serious crime in the modern therapeutic world: he had challenged the dominant narrative of the trans revolution and called into question whether it really was delivering on the promises it made.

The banning of Anderson's book, like the Bostock ruling and the Biden executive order, have implications for all of us. Amazon has a vice-like grip on book sales in the United States and increasingly elsewhere. A book denied a platform at Amazon is a book likely to be far less attractive to a publisher as a product or, indeed, to an author as a project. This is not old-style censorship by governments, of the kind that characterized the Soviet Union. It is censorship via corporate, economic power. But it is censorship nonetheless, here in the service of trans ideology but with potential implications for anything with which the Amazon executives care to disagree.

Conclusion

The sexual revolution of the LGBTQ+ is fascinating because it represents the outworking of sexualized expressive individualism in public life. It also highlights where the sexual revolution is tending. The L, the G, and the B now look remarkably passé, assuming as they do the importance of biological sex for the gender binary. The T and the Q, denying this, have proved both parasitic upon the gains made by the LGB and ultimately destructive of the LGB, as well as of traditional feminism. The civil wars we now see opening up on the left over trans ideology bear witness to this.

More significant, however, is the fact that these radical forms of expressive individualism, allied to powerful narratives of victimhood and oppression, are set to change all of our lives. It is to that we turn in the next chapter, where we will see that two of the most unquestioned freedoms of Western liberal democracy, those of speech and religion, are now in serious jeopardy.

Study Questions

1. How have these gender laws and cultural changes affected your work?

2. How will you stand firm in your belief system?

3. What are the implications of trans ideology for biological females in the public sphere? What about for males?

4. In what ways do traditional gender norms create a flourishing society?

5. Discuss the potential negative impacts on children of a society filled with gender confusion and trans ideology. How will their identities, mental health, and perspective on life be affected?

Life, Liberty, and the Pursuit of Happiness

Introduction

The United States Declaration of Independence declares that "life, liberty, and the pursuit of happiness" are inalienable human rights. While the document is distinctively American, and times have changed since Jefferson first put quill to paper, it is surely the case that these three things capture in a beautifully concise form the dominant Western approach to what it means to be human. We prize life; we consider personal freedom of central importance; and who does not want to be happy?

Yet the rise of expressive individualism, of the normative modern "self" described in this book, means that all three categories have changed somewhat in terms of their actual content or definition. Indeed, given the assumption that these are distinctively human concerns, it makes perfect sense that as the nature of what it means to be human has changed, so this has had significant implications for how life, freedom, and happiness are to be understood.

Modern Life

Expressive individualism has a profound impact on matters of life and death for several reasons. First, it tends to lead us to think about personhood as being something that requires a degree of self-consciousness. If the self is defined by how we think, feel, and desire, then we need to be at a stage of intellectual development where these things can take place in order to be a true person. And that shapes how we understand issues surrounding the beginning and end of life.

This is exemplified in the work of Peter Singer, the Princeton University ethicist. Singer is comfortable with acknowledging embryos as possessing life, but he denies that they are persons. For him, to be a person is to be self-conscious and that means one must have the ability to express oneself, to conceptualize and to act intentionally toward the future, and to act deliberately in ways that further one's own happiness. These are things that embryos cannot do. Indeed, newborn babies and adults with advanced dementia, among others, are also incapable of such things and therefore lack true personhood—and the rights typically enjoyed by persons.

This then leads to a second implication: ethics of life and death in a world of expressive individualism tend to default to a form of utilitarianism. Utilitarianism is the philosophy of life where the morally defensible position is that which gives most happiness to most of the persons involved. Therefore, if a child in the womb, or even a newborn baby, has Down syndrome or a birth defect, that is something that may well have an adverse effect upon the parents' happiness. It means that their lives will be considerably transformed by the presence of the child. They will have responsibilities that they would otherwise not have; and perhaps the joy of having a child will be highly qualified, if not negated, by the child's long-term, radical dependency upon them. In this case, abortion or even euthanasia after birth, can be justified because the net amount of happiness for the persons involved (only the adults, not the newborn) will be greater if the child is killed. Not being a person, it has no personal rights.

The same applies to those with advanced dementia: having lost their mental faculties, they have therefore lost their personhood. Whether to keep them alive becomes a matter of the happiness of the healthy family members responsible for their care. Once that continued existence becomes a burden on such and begins to lower their level of happiness, euthanizing the patient is not murder but a moral act, perhaps even an imperative one.

Similar utilitarian logic lies behind the rising acceptance, even legalization, of assisted suicide in Western countries: when a person decides that life is no longer worth living, whether because of physical illness or mental distress, life can be terminated. Perhaps the most obvious cases of recent years have involved those with terminal medical conditions such as cancer, but they need not be restricted to that. In the world of psychologized selfhood in which we all now live, mental suffering can also be claimed as a criterion for euthanasia. While the legal situation on this remains somewhat murky, it is easy to imagine that euthanasia for those who are severely depressed could easily become a plausible, even accepted, part of our culture.

Modern Liberty

While the speed of the sexual revolution has been shocking to many, perhaps the strangest and most disturbing developments over recent years have been the ways in which freedoms once considered to be self-evident goods—of speech and of religion—are now under pressure in many Western democracies. This is something both unexpected and sinister.

Growing up in Britain in the 1970s and '80s, I was taught that the freedom to speak as one pleased and to worship— or not—as one chose were two of the primary things that made Western society better than the totalitarian regimes of the Soviet Union and China. If anyone had said to me that within my own lifetime these liberties would become highly contested within Western society and even be seen as either irrelevant or deeply problematic by significant numbers of people, I would have been shocked. Yet this is the point at which we now find ourselves. When I was young, religious people were often regarded as foolish or hypocritical by the wider culture, but I do not recall any widespread belief that they were, as a class, dangerous, hate-filled bigots who represented a threat to civil order. And assaults on freedom of speech, such as the infamous edict issued by the Ayatollah Khomeini against the British author Salman Rushdie for the alleged blasphemy of his book *The Satanic Verses*, were met with near universal abhorrence and condemnation in the West. Now, scarcely a week goes by without some tale of "cancel culture" and of a person being harangued into silence on social media for the articulation of a view that was considered unexceptionable until very recently.

The reasons for this change and for these attacks on traditional freedoms are rooted in the narrative of the self that we have been tracing in this book. Knowing the story of the modern self makes the assaults on traditional freedoms, if not the inevitable, then certainly an explicable, outcome.

The Problem with Religion

There is a clear connection between the sexual revolution and the growing antipathy evident in our culture toward freedom of religion. Perhaps the first time this caught the news headlines was in early 2015 when the Indiana state legislature proposed a Religious Freedom Restoration Act that was in part designed to protect the rights of business owners with religious objections to LGBTQ+ lifestyles with regard to hiring policies. The proposal met with swift and widespread condemnation, most significantly from corporate America, on the grounds that, if passed, it would allow such religious businesspeople to discriminate against LGBTQ+ employees. In the end, then–Indiana governor, Mike Pence, signed a watered-down version of the original bill into law. But a message had been sent: significant sectors of the culture no longer considered religious objections to LGBTQ+ matters to be anything more than bigotry, and policies based on such no more than pandering.

In fact, this position was already clear in a significant ruling of the United States Supreme Court in 2013, that of *United States v. Windsor*. The background was the Defense of Marriage Act (DOMA), signed into law by President Clinton in 1996. This legislation specifically excluded same-sex partnerships from the state-recognized definition of marriage. DOMA, however, came under challenge by a woman named Edith Windsor. In 2007, Windsor had married her same-sex partner, Thea Spyer, in Canada. The couple lived in New York state, and when Spyer died in 2009, Windsor tried to claim the federal estate tax exemption to which legally recognized spouses are entitled. This claim was denied under the terms of section 3 of DOMA, which excluded same-sex partnerships, and

Windsor sued. Her claim was upheld by both a district court and the Court of Appeals for the Second Circuit in 2012. Then, with the case pending for the Supreme Court, the Justice Department announced that it would not seek to defend DOMA. At this point, a bipartisan legal advisory group of the House of Representatives voted to take up the suit with a view to determining the constitutionality of section 3, which defined marriage as being between a man and a woman.

The Supreme Court ruled, by a 5–4 majority, that section 3 was not constitutional and thereby overthrew the central principle of DOMA, that marriage was to be exclusively understood as between one man and one woman. Public attitudes on the issue were already shifting, and so the decision was not a complete shock. What was surprising, however, was the way in which the court's majority characterized the motive of the opponents of gay marriage that underlay DOMA. The relevant passage reads as follows:

DOMA's unusual deviation from the usual tradition of recognizing and accepting state definitions of marriage here operates to deprive same-sex couples of the benefits and responsibilities that come with the federal recognition of their marriages. This is strong evidence of a law having the purpose and effect of disapproval of that class. The avowed purpose and practical effect of the law here in question are to impose a disadvantage, a separate status, and so a stigma upon all who enter into same-sex marriages made lawful by the unquestioned authority of the States.[1]

From this it is clear that the court saw the objections to gay marriage as being grounded in what is technically termed constitutional animus or, to put the same idea in more colloquial terms, irrational bigotry.

It is worth reflecting on that for a moment. Christians—and Jews—hold to a view of marriage that sees it as being between one man and one woman, and that for numerous reasons: the teaching of Genesis 2, the complementarity of men and women, and the procreative intention of marriage. Yet in Windsor, the Supreme Court dismisses two thousand years of Christian thinking (and many more of Jewish thought) as nothing more than irrational bigotry. At best, the court presumably decided that even if religious objections to gay marriage had once had validity, they did so no longer and the only reason for maintaining such was a smokescreen for justifying the marginalization of a certain sector of society. When the highest court in the land can codify such a view of religion in a judgment, the times—and the cultural attitudes—have truly changed.

Windsor provided the immediate legal background to *Obergefell v. Hodges*, 576 U.S. 644 (2015), the Supreme Court case that found same-sex marriage to be protected by the Constitution on grounds consistent with the expressive individualism we have been tracing. Foundational to this finding was the Court's assertion of the autonomy of individuals in being able to choose whom they wanted to marry. This reflected a position established in law in an earlier decision, *Planned Parenthood of Southeastern Pennsylvania v. Casey*, 505 U.S. 833, 851 (1992), in which Planned Parenthood had challenged a law signed by then–Pennsylvania governor, Robert Casey Sr., that imposed certain restrictions on the provision of abortions. The ruling went against Casey, but the interesting part of the judgment was a bizarre but subsequently influential statement by the author of the majority opinion, Justice Anthony Kennedy, in which he described what it is to be a person:

At the heart of liberty is the right to define one's own concept of existence, of meaning, of the universe, and of the mystery of human life. Beliefs about these matters could not define the attributes of personhood were they formed under compulsion of the State.[2]

Kennedy captures here the very essence of expressive individualism and its implications: individuals can define for themselves what gives them their identity, their purpose in life, and their sense of meaning. With that established as the basic assumption of American constitutional law, the foundation was laid for the later rulings on marriage that saw its restriction to one man and one woman as oppressive, as bigotry, and as hindering personal autonomy and happiness. Gay marriage may not have been inevitable in 1992, but this ruling certainly cleared the ground for it.

Not Tolerance, but Equality

Given the above, it should be clear that tolerance of LGBTQ+ identities was never going to be enough for the movement. To tolerate somebody is, by definition, to disapprove of them, albeit in a rather passive way. But it is also not to recognize them, as we defined recognition earlier: it is not to affirm their identities as they wish to be affirmed; at best, it is to keep them in place as second-class members of society.

And this in turn helps to explain the reason why such things as cake baking have become so contentious. The Christian baker who refuses to produce a cake for a gay marriage celebration is doing so because her conscience would regard such an act as supporting a relationship she regards as fundamentally immoral. The gay couple, however, regard her refusal as a denial of their fundamental (and constitutionally protected) identity. Equality requires equal recognition of a kind that tolerance simply does not provide.

This tracks back, of course, to the modern, psychological construction of identity. If we are above all what we think, what we feel, what we desire, then anything that interferes or obstructs those thoughts, feelings, or desires, inhibits us as people and prevents us from being the self that we are convinced that we are. Such obstructions inhibit identity in a deep and substantial way. Verbal insults, of course, are nothing new and have a history as long as that of humanity itself. Goliath mocked David. Cicero insulted Catiline. But with the rise of the psychological self, words have taken on a new cultural power, as witnessed by the fierce debates that now rage over pronouns. The use of a word deemed hurtful or denigrating becomes in the world of psychological identity an assault upon the person, as real in its own way as a blow from a fist.

And this is where religions, especially religions such as Christianity and Judaism that hold to strict codes with regard to sex and sexuality, will end up in trouble because they are going to find themselves in a world that operates with what we might call a different grammar and syntax of identity. For example, when the Christian objects to homosexuality, he may well think he is objecting to a set of sexual desires or sexual practices. But the gay man sees those desires as part of who he is in his very essence. The old chestnut of "love the sinner, hate the sin" simply does not work in a world where the sin is the identity of the sinner and the two cannot be separated even at a conceptual level. In a time when the normative notion of selfhood is psychological, then to hate the sin is to hate the sinner. Christians who fail to note this shift are going to find themselves very confused by the incomprehension of, and indeed the easy offence taken by, the world around them.

In his *Notes on the State of Virginia*, Thomas Jefferson famously commented that "it does me no injury for my neighbour to say there are twenty gods, or no god. It neither picks my pocket nor breaks my leg." For Jefferson, this was why freedom of religion was not a complicated matter: the personal religious beliefs of others did not damage him financially or harm him physically. In terms of the argument of this book, we might infer, therefore, that Jefferson was living in a world where selfhood was not so psychologically constructed but tied far more closely to the physical, to the individual's body and property. But that does not apply today: in a world where inner psychology dominates how we think of ourselves, then feelings too become very important in how we conceptualize harm. In that world, the personal religious beliefs of our neighbors are of concern because disagreement implies that at least one of us is wrong. And today, that constitutes a form of oppression. Pockets may not be picked and legs may not be broken by religious conservatives, but feelings are hurt and identities are therefore marginalized, oppressed, and denied legitimacy.

The Problem with Free Speech

It should be clear from the above that the problem that is pressing against religious freedom is not restricted to religion. Indeed, the challenge to religious freedom is simply the specific instance of a much broader challenge to traditional freedom of speech. Religious speech is problematic precisely because words in general have come to take on new significance in this psychologized world. And nowhere has this challenge emerged more unexpectedly and with more drama than on college campuses, the very places where freedom of speech and inquiry would seem so basic to the educational task.

Now, the First Amendment of the United States Constitution protects freedom of speech but does not do so without qualification. The classic example of this is the famous paraphrase of Judge Oliver Wendell Holmes's ruling in *Schenck v. United States* (1919) that mischievously shouting "Fire!" in a crowded theater is not protected under the First Amendment.[3] Another Supreme Court judgment, in *Brandenburg v. Ohio* (1969) further ruled that speech likely to cause imminent lawless action was likewise not protected.[4] Even so, these rulings indicate that the First Amendment offers very broad protections to speech and thus to the public expression of a wide variety of views, any number of which might be found disagreeable or even reprehensible by sections of the population. I might well consider someone's views on abortion or sexuality to be offensive, but unless those views are expressed with the intention of inciting immediate violence, the person expressing them has every right to do so.

When violence moves from the physical and the financial to the psychological, however, everything changes. Once oppression is seen to exist in its most insidious form at the level of psychology, at the point where culture shapes the individual's ideas and intuitions, then a different notion of political freedom inevitably emerges. While many traditional conservatives and liberals are shocked at the current push against freedom of speech, it makes sense given the broader changes in society's notion of the self.

A theoretical harbinger of this was set forth by the New Left philosopher Herbert Marcuse in a controversial 1965 essay, "Repressive Tolerance."[5] Marcuse, a member of the Frankfurt School, was a Marxist thinker who had drawn heavily upon the thought of Sigmund Freud in order to formulate his political philosophy. As with Reich (see chapter 4), Marcuse was concerned with why people did not develop a revolutionary self-consciousness but were often gulled into accepting the status quo. In "Repressive Tolerance," Marcuse presents the traditional liberal concept of freedom of speech as a confidence trick that gives the impression that true freedom exists. The ruling class officially allows freedom of speech and expression while quietly imposing severe limits on that freedom. For example, he notes that in a Western democracy, one can freely advocate Marxism as a set of ideas, but if one moves toward enacting such (inevitably by a seriously disruptive, even violent challenge to the status quo), then one would find such freedom rapidly curtailed by the dominant political powers. Freedom of speech as a broad, unqualified principle is thus for Marcuse something akin to the old "bread and circuses" of the Roman Empire. It is a way of distracting people from seeing the real injustices of the world in which they live.

In articulating this principle, Marcuse offers an analysis that has obvious significance for our current situation in the practical conclusions it draws for those wishing to engage in a true and just transformation of society:

> When tolerance mainly serves the protection and preservation of a repressive society, when it serves to neutralize opposition and to render men immune against other and better forms of life, then tolerance has been perverted. And when this perversion starts in the mind of the individual, in his consciousness, his needs, when heteronomous interests occupy him before he can experience his servitude, then the efforts to counteract his dehumanization must begin at the place of entrance, there where the false consciousness takes form (or rather: is systematically formed)—it must begin with stopping the words and images

which feed this consciousness. To be sure, this is censorship, even precensorship, but openly directed against the more or less hidden censorship that permeates the free media.[6]

What Marcuse is calling for here is the censoring of speech as a means of moving society toward a more just and equitable state. To allow speech that presents the injustices of the status quo—economic, sexual, racial, etc.—as legitimate or even natural is to offer support to those injustices. It therefore behooves the left, of which Marcuse is of course the spokesperson, to work toward closing down the avenues and opportunities for such speech.

We should note that this goes well beyond the use of pejorative epithets. Most people acknowledge that the use of certain words such as racial epithets is wrong (even if they might still defend the freedom of people to use such). But the Marcusan perspective does not simply call for the outlawing of particularly insulting words and phrases. It is also a call for a much more thorough policing of speech, one that includes philosophies and worldviews as well. Indeed, we might rephrase Marcuse by saying that he wants narratives that run contrary to his vision of society to be outlawed on the grounds that they present a false view of reality and serve to dehumanize people.

To bring this into the language of the present day, there are those who offer narratives that reinforce attitudes and systems which are considered by those on the left to be unjust. Such people need to be silenced and their narratives censured and censored. Therefore, if someone is seen to be speaking in a way that perpetuates the normative status of heterosexual white males and thereby explicitly or implicitly marginalizing others—LGBTQ+ people, women, ethnic minorities, etc.—such speech is to be suppressed by any means necessary. This is why we now see battles over speech codes on campuses, in the workplace, and even in the public square.

Given the narrative of the psychological self, this all makes perfect sense. If human happiness is constituted by an inner sense of well-being, then anything that disrupts that is problematic. The implications of this are dramatic and set to be comprehensive, or at least to involve all areas of the public square.

Take, for example, education. Traditional notions of education assumed that students were raw material in need of training which would shape them into adult members of society by imparting skills and knowledge necessary for fitting in to the larger social framework that is the adult world. This vision was not simply technical: liberal arts education also saw the teaching of the great classics of culture—literature, art, music, philosophy—as shaping the student's understanding of what it means to be human. To be educated was to be transformed by exposure to a range of ideas, whether one agreed with them or not.

Once society accepts the basic Rousseau-style premise, that culture is what makes us inauthentic by perverting the voice of nature, and then refracts this through the critical lenses provided by Nietzsche, Marx, Freud, and the New Left of Reich and Marcuse, this traditional notion of education must be abandoned. History, for example, becomes a tale of oppression, not a source for contemporary wisdom. It is something that must be overcome, not something to be embraced and upon which we can build. And the free exchange of ideas comes to seem more like the legitimation of bigotry and ignorance than the foundation for good citizenship.

One of the most notorious examples of this occurred at Middlebury College in March 2017, where the sociologist Charles Murray was invited to speak to the student chapter of the American

Enterprise Institute. Earlier in his career, Murray had co-authored a book, *The Bell Curve*, in which he had argued that intelligence played a role in the economic divisions within American society. Such a view was regarded by his critics, of whom there were many among the students at Middlebury, as justifying racial and class prejudice. The invitation provoked campus protests that degenerated into a violent confrontation in which Allison Stanger, the left-leaning faculty member who had agreed to respond to Murray, was injured.

The Middlebury incident was violent and unpleasant but also consistent with an emerging discomfort on college campuses with the traditional notion of freedom of speech. Old-style liberals considered such a freedom to be a vital component of a free society, on the basis that the best antidote to bad ideas is a context where good ideas can compete freely with such in the public square. New style progressives, however, have increasingly argued that freedom of speech is really a means of allowing bigotry and hatred to be expressed with impunity and treated as legitimate viewpoints. One website associated with Middlebury students expressed the matter as follows:

> We feel as though individually, our voices are often ignored in the face of the hegemonic Middlebury discourse, but collectively we will be able to engage with the Middlebury community more effectively. We are a radical, anti-racist, anti-sexist, anti-classist, anti-ableist, and anti-homophobic (as well as strongly opposed to all forms of oppression) group that rejects the structurally conservative "liberal" paradigm that exists at Middlebury. The reasons behind our formation are many, but the predominate [sic] one is a feeling of alienation within the campus dialogue—

the so-called "free market of ideas" on campus is an illusion, one which exists only to support one strong ideology.[7]

Notice that final sentence: freedom of speech on campus is identified with the reinforcement and maintenance of one specific ideology, by inference a racist, sexist, classist, ableist, and homophobic one. Given that academics have in recent years been dismissed for infelicitous tweets, it is hard to imagine a liberal arts college in twenty-first-century America where racist views are the staple of classroom teaching. But that is the claim being made because in the world of psychologized selfhood, society's modern politically-favored identities see any challenge to them—in fact, any failure to affirm them fully and wholeheartedly—as assaults on their legitimacy.

While the Middlebury incident grabbed the headlines because of its violent drama, a more peaceful but in many ways far more significant transformation of the higher educational curriculum, at least in the humanities, has been gathering pace for some years. A glance at the website of Harvard University's History Department indicates that once-central themes for the historical discipline such as the Reformation and the Renaissance have been relativized and abbreviated while others, such as pornography, feminism, and colonial violence, have emerged. As I write this, the University of Oxford is considering calls to revise its music curriculum on the grounds that it has been too preoccupied with white, European composers and genres. And these examples are not outliers or exceptional. A broad rebellion against traditional curricular canons in the humanities seems to be afoot in higher education on both sides of the Atlantic.

To be sure, these "canon wars" are not without merit. As a historian, I welcome the advent of approaches to history that bring attention to marginalized voices. Marxists such as E. P. Thompson made significant contributions by highlighting the role of the working classes. African American history has done sterling service in pointing out that the history of the United States cannot be told simply from the perspective of white males, with everyone else playing little more than bit parts. Slavery shaped—and its legacy continues to shape—the experience of African Americans in the United States. The voices of people of color are a vital part of the American story, both for offering perspectives on the dark side of American history as well as enriching discussion of one of the key motifs of the American experiment: the ideal of freedom and how it has, or has not, been consistently realized in American culture. And all historians should welcome challenges to their own viewpoints and interpretations. That is how we grow in our knowledge of the past and of what it means to be human. The expansion of the canon to include the previously dispossessed and ignored can only enrich the historical discipline, as it can other disciplines such as literature and music.

The problem, of course, is that the purpose of these canon wars is not to expand the canon but to replace it, or, perhaps more accurately, shatter the very concept of canon as being inherently exclusionary and oppressive. It is not that traditional courses on the Reformation or on Beethoven are to have their bibliographies supplemented or to have other courses coordinated with them. It is the very notion of having a course on the Reformation or on Beethoven—let alone making such courses central, core parts of the curriculum—that the post-Marcuse world challenges as elitist and smelling of white, heterosexual, male privilege.

And while this may look like left-wing political gerrymandering of the curriculum, it has potency not because the wider world has bought into New Left forms of Marxism and cultural transformation but because it has bought into psychologized selfhood and expressive individualism. The claim that certain narratives are psychologically oppressive is plausible to many because our modern intuitions are to see ourselves as psychological beings and anything that obstructs our psychological happiness, our sense of self, is inevitably bad, oppressive, and something to be opposed. Victimhood has an intrinsic virtue to it; and anything that can lay claim to the vocabulary of the victim has unlocked a major, even irresistible, source of cultural power. Freedom of speech and academic freedom are simply licenses to oppress and marginalize the weak. True freedom is found in closing down such traditional virtues and replacing them with a victim-centered authoritarianism.

Conclusion

The impact of expressive individualism on how we think about life and liberty has been dramatic. Old notions such as the sanctity of life and the importance of freedom of religion and speech have been transformed, even inverted, by this new, modern self. And all this is because the notion of happiness with which we now intuitively operate is one where a sense of personal, psychological well-being is central. We might say that happiness is for each of us first and foremost an individual thing, resting upon us being independent; all other relationships must serve that end or be seen as oppressive.

Ironically, this has led to a most strange and counterintuitive situation. While our notion of identity has become one where we are self-creators whose self-creations are not to be judged or criticized by others, it is clear that some identities must inevitably stand over against or in contradiction to each other. The existence of the traditional Christian is a threat to the person who identifies as transgender; the person who teaches Western civilization is a threat to the person whose identity is framed by the repudiation of the colonialist past. And that means that somebody has to make the decision as to which of these incommensurable and contradictory identities is to be given legitimacy in society and which are to be suppressed, outlawed, and banished.

And so we have an ironic situation at present: radical individual freedom has led to rather authoritarian forms of social control, from elementary schools that teach gender ideology to Ivy League schools that have abandoned traditional curricula, from workplaces that require sensitivity training on transgender issues to big tech giants boycotting states because of religious freedom legislation passed by democratically elected assemblies, from local schoolboards pressing ideological uniformity via the rhetoric of diversity to national governments broadening civil rights legislation to protect chaotic views of gender.

All of this obviously has serious implications for the church, for orthodox Christians, and for religiously and culturally conservative and traditional people in general. The world where freedom of religion, let alone freedom of speech, is now regarded by some (many?) as a problem for a free society rather than a basic foundation of the same is indeed a strange new world. But, strange and new as it is, it is also our world, the one to which we are called to respond. What such a response might look like, or in what it might consist, is the subject of the next and final chapter.

Study Questions

1. In what areas of life may you have been tempted to think in utilitarian ways, and what aspects of our culture cause that temptation?

2. What important aspects of history as we know it do we stand to lose by allowing expressive individualism to reconstruct the canon?

3. What does the future look like for white, heterosexual males given the influence of expressive individualism on the modern world?

4. How could you be "cancelled" in today's culture?

Strangers in This Strange New World

Introduction

For traditional Christians, the narrative of this book is inevitably a somewhat depressing one, as it points both to past transformations in the notion of selfhood that challenge our views at every level and indicates that the world in which we now live is hostile to expression of our beliefs on these matters. To object to same-sex marriage, for example, is in the moral register of the day not substantially different from being a racist. The era when Christians could disagree with the broader convictions of the secular world and yet still find themselves respected as decent members of society at large is coming to an end, if indeed it has not ended already. The truth is that the last vestiges of a social imaginary shaped by Christianity are rapidly vanishing, and many of us are even now living as strangers in a strange new world. The revolution in self-hood, particularly as it manifests itself in the various facets of the sexual revolution, is set to exert pressure on the lives of all of us, from kindergarten education to workplace policies on pronouns. Christians might still be able to run, so to speak, and avoid some of these things for some period of time, but they cannot hide forever. Sooner or later every single one of us is likely to be faced with a challenging situation generated by the modern notion of selfhood. And this means that for all of us the questions of how we should live, and what we should do when facing pressure to conform, are gaining in urgency.

Understanding Our Complicity

The first thing that we need to do is understand our complicity in the expressive individualism of our day. This statement needs a little nuance, however, because expressive individualism is not all bad. We do have feelings; we do have an inner psychological space that deeply shapes who we are. Historically, while Rousseau is developing his notion of the self as rooted in inner sentiments, so Jonathan Edwards is writing *Religious Affections* and exploring that inner space from an explicitly Christian perspective. Expressive individualism is correct in affirming the importance of psychology for who we are and in stressing the universal dignity of all human beings. We might also add that this accenting of the individual is consonant with the existential urgency of the New Testament in the way it stresses the importance of personal faith as a response to the gospel. Only I can believe for me. And that places the "I" in a most important place.

But there are also problems here. Think, for example, of freedom of religion. This is a social virtue. What Christian wants to live in a country where the church is persecuted and where worshiping God is considered a crime? Yet countries where there is such freedom are also typically countries where there are many churches, even religions, to which one can choose to belong. Within ten miles of where I am writing this book in my study at home in Pennsylvania, there are dozens of churches—Presbyterian, Lutheran, Eastern Orthodox, Baptist, Roman Catholic. And even the terms "Presbyterian," "Lutheran," and "Baptist" cover a variety of different denominations. This is the result of religious freedom—a good thing—but it also has the effect of making religion a marketplace where the congregant is the customer and the church the vendor. This means that the authority in religion tilts toward the congregant, the customer, in a way that panders to the felt needs of the psychological self.

To make the point more sharply, it is worth noting a comment once made by Philip Rieff: "Formerly, if men were miserable, they went to church, so as to find the rationale of their misery; they did not expect to be happy, this idea is Greek, not Christian or Jewish."[1] Such a notion is incomprehensible today: we as Christians intuitively go to church to feel good—perhaps to meet friends or to sing uplifting songs (whether traditional or contemporary) or to have our minds stimulated by a good sermon or our ears edified by beautiful music. Prayers, personal and corporate, tend to focus on the alleviation of misery, not being enabled to understand it. We tend to go to—to choose!—the church that fits with what makes us personally feel good. This is true whether we are, say, emotional types to whom a Pentecostal service might appeal; lovers of artistic beauty, who might be naturally drawn to high Anglicanism, Catholicism, or Orthodoxy; or (like me) a bookish type, for whom the cerebral sermons of Reformed churches are appealing.

Perhaps I have overstated things here. But most of us, if we are honest with ourselves, would have to admit that our choice of church is not entirely driven by theological conviction. Personal taste plays a role, and that is shaped by the expectations of the psychologized, therapeutic society in which we live, move, and have our being.

This also connects to another way in which the church has become more akin to the world than she often realizes: the cult of personal happiness. Now, there is nothing wrong with being happy, of course. But as we noted in the last chapter, the nature of happiness has changed over the years to being akin to an inner sense of psychological well-being. Once we start thinking of happiness in those terms, the vision of the Christian life laid out in Paul's letters, particularly 2 Corinthians, becomes incomprehensible. We may not all be explicitly committed to the prosperity gospel, but many of us think of divine blessing in terms of our individual happiness. That is a result of the psychological, therapeutic culture seeping into our Christianity.

There are other areas of Christian complicity as well. How many churches have taken a firm stand on no-fault divorce, a concept predicated on a view of marriage that sees it as being of no significance once the personal happiness of one or both parties is not being met? How many Christians allow their emotions to govern their ethics when a beloved relative or friend comes out as gay or transgender? We are all complicit at some level in the world I have described in this book.

How we can address this is not easy to see, but a few thoughts suggest themselves. First, we need to examine ourselves, individually and corporately, to see in what ways we have compromised the gospel with the spirit of this age. Then, we need to repent, call out to the Lord for grace, and seek to reform our beliefs, attitudes, intuitions, and practices accordingly. Nothing less is required for a true reformation at this point.

Second, an awareness of our complicity should cultivate a level of humility in how we engage with those with whom we disagree on these matters. There can be no place for the pharisaic prayer whereby we thank the Lord that we are not like other men.

Third, to be aware of our complicity at least allows us to engage in the future in appropriate self-criticism and self-policing on such issues. We cannot help but choose the church in which we worship. Even the cradle Catholic today chooses to continue to attend church because there are many other available options, including not attending church at all. But having chosen the church, we can discipline ourselves to be committed to that church, to stick with it, to refuse to allow ourselves to move on simply because of some trivial issue or matter of personal taste. This will be far from perfect and far from easy, but I see no other option than self-awareness and self-discipline in this matter.

Learn from the Ancient Church

Traditional Christians are typically those who take history seriously. We have a faith rooted in historical claims (supremely the incarnation of Jesus Christ and the events and actions of his life) and see our religious communities as standing in a line extending back through time to Pentecost and beyond. Thus, when faced with peculiar challenges, Christians often look to the past to find hope with regard to their experience in the present. Typically, Protestants look to the Reformation, and Catholics look to the High Middle Ages. If only we might be able to return to that world, we tell ourselves, all might be well.

Anyone with a realistic sense of history knows that such returns are at best virtually impossible. First, neither the Reformation nor the High Middle Ages were the golden eras that later religious nostalgia would have us believe. The societies in which the church operated in those periods are gone forever, thanks in large part to the ways in which technology has reshaped the world in which we now live.

If we are to find a precedent for our times, I believe that we must go further back in time, to the second century and the immediately post-apostolic church. There, Christianity was a little-understood, despised, marginal sect. It was suspected of being immoral and seditious. Eating the body and blood of their god and calling each other "brother" and "sister" even when married made Christians and Christianity sound highly dubious to outsiders. And the claim that "Jesus is Lord!" was on the surface a pledge of loyalty that derogated from that owed to Caesar. That is much like the situation of the church today. For example, we are considered irrational bigots for our stance on gay marriage. In the aftermath of the Trump presidency, it has become routine to hear religious conservatives in general, and evangelical Christians in particular, decried as representing a threat to civil society. Like our spiritual ancestors in the second century, we too are deemed immoral and seditious.

Of course, the analogy is not perfect. The church in the second century faced a pagan world that had never known Christianity. We live in a world that is de-Christianizing, often self-consciously and intentionally. That means that the opposition is likely better informed and more proactive than in the ancient church. Yet a glance at the church's strategy in the second century is still instructive.

First, it is clear from the New Testament and from early non-canonical texts like the *Didache* that community was central to church life. The Acts of the Apostles presents a picture of a church where Christians cared for and served each other. The *Didache* sets forth a set of moral prescriptions, including a ban on abortion and infanticide, that served to distinguish the church from the world around. Christian identity was clearly a very practical, down-to-earth, and day-to-day thing.

This makes perfect sense. Underlying much of the argument of previous chapters—indeed, underlying the notion of the social imaginary—is that identity is shaped by the communities to which we belong. And we all have various identities—I am a husband, a father, a teacher, an Englishman, an immigrant, a writer, a rugby fan, in addition to being a Christian. And the strongest identities I have, forming my strongest intuitions, derive from the strongest communities to which I belong. And that means that the church needs to be the strongest community to which we each belong.

Ironically, the LGBTQ+ community is proof of this point: the reason they have moved from the margins to center stage is intimately connected to the strong communities they formed while on the margins. This is why lamentation for Christianity's cultural marginalization, while legitimate, cannot be the sole response of the church to the current social convulsions she is experiencing. Lament, for sure—we should lament that the world is not as it should be, as many of the Psalms teach us—but also organize. Become a community. By this, the Lord says, shall all men know that you are my disciples, by the love you have for each other (John 13:35). And that means community.

This brings me to the second lesson we can learn from the early church. Community in terms of its day-to-day details might look different in a city from in a rural village, or in the United States from in the United Kingdom. But there are certain elements that the church in every place will share: worship and fellowship. Gathering together on the Lord's Day, praying, singing God's praise, hearing the word read and preached, celebrating baptism and the Lord's Supper, giving materially to the church's work—these are things all Christians should do when gathered together. It might sound trite, but a large part of the church's witness to the world is simply being the church in worship. Paul himself comments that when an unbeliever accidentally turns up at a church service, he should be struck by the otherworldly holiness of what is going on. The most powerful witness to the gospel is the church herself, simply going about the business of worship.

Many Christians talk of engaging the culture. In fact, the culture is most dramatically engaged by the church presenting it with another culture, another form of community, rooted in her liturgical worship practices and manifested in the loving community that exists both in and beyond the worship service. Many talk of the culture war between Christians and secularism, and certainly the Bible itself uses martial language to describe the spiritual conflict of this present age. But perhaps "cultural protest" is a way of better translating that idea into modern idiom, given the reality and history of physical warfare in our world. The church protests the wider culture by offering a true vision of what it means to be a human being made in the image of God.

This approach is certainly hinted at in second-century Christian literature. The so-called Greek Apologists, such as Justin Martyr, addressed the Roman Empire from a Christian perspective. What is so interesting when compared to some of the ways many Christians, right and left, do so today is how respectful these ancient apologists were. They did not spend their time denouncing the evils of the emperor and his court. Rather, they argued positively that Christians made the best citizens, the best parents, the best servants, the best neighbors, the best employees, and that they should thus be left alone and allowed to carry on with their day-to-day lives without being harassed by the authorities. Of course, there were limits to what they could do to participate in civic life: if asked to sacrifice to the emperor as to a god, they would have to refuse, but beyond such demands, they could be good members of the Roman community.

In the fifth century, Augustine in Book XIX of his masterpiece *The City of God* offered a similar argument. Christians, he said, were citizens of both the earthly city and the city of God. Their pagan neighbors might only be citizens of the earthly city, but this still meant that the two groups shared common interests or loves, above all the peace and prosperity of the earthly city. Both pagans and Christians wanted these things and could work together to achieve them. And that meant that Christians could and should be good citizens to the extent that their higher commitment to God allowed them to do so.[2]

The Apologists and Augustine both offer a vision of the church in a hostile culture that calls on the church to be the church and on Christians to be constructive members of the wider society in which they are placed. Some might respond that failing to engage in aggressive and direct confrontation looks rather like defeatism or withdrawal. But is it? On key issues such as abortion, Christians in the West are still at liberty to use their rights as members of the earthly city to campaign for the good. I am not here calling for a kind of passive quietism whereby Christians abdicate their civic responsibilities or make no connection between how to pursue those civic responsibilities and their religious beliefs. I am suggesting rather that engaging in cultural warfare using the world's tools, rhetoric, and weapons is not the way for God's people. If the Apologists and Augustine were passive quietists, it is rather hard to explain how Christianity came to be so dominant in the West for so many centuries. The historical evidence suggests rather that their approach proved remarkably effective over time. And so it may again—perhaps not in my lifetime or even in that of my children. But God is sovereign, God plays the long game, and God's will shall be done, on earth as it is heaven.

Teach the Whole Counsel of God

One of the temptations at a time of tremendous flux and change is to fixate upon the immediate challenges to the Christian faith. Now, it is surely not a bad thing to prioritize the most pressing problems the church faces and address them with a degree of urgency. The sale of indulgences, for example, was a major problem in 1517, and it was right for Luther to focus on that, rather than spend his time writing on the issue of same-sex marriage, a matter of no import whatsoever in the early sixteenth century. Yet there is a danger here: we can become so preoccupied with specific threats that we neglect the important fact that Christian truth is not a set of isolated and unconnected claims but rather stands as a coherent whole. The church's teaching on gender, marriage, and sex is a function of her teaching on what it means to be human. The doctrines of creation, fall, redemption, and consummation are important foundations for addressing the specific challenges of our time. If, as I have argued in this book, modern sexual and identity politics are functions of deeper notions of selfhood, then we need first to know what the Christian view of the self is in order to address them. And as the Bible teaches that the human self is made in the image of God, we need a good grasp of the doctrine of God. In short, we can stand strong at this cultural moment and address the specific challenges we face only if our foundations in God's truth are broad and deep.

This means that the chaotic nature of our times is no excuse for abandoning the church's task of teaching her people the whole counsel of God. If anything, she should see such a moment as a time to examine whether that is what she is doing and make any necessary changes in her pedagogical strategy. She needs to make sure that Christians are being intentionally grounded in the truth. As with community, the strategy for doing this might look different in different places and congregations, but I would suggest that the use of a good historical confession or catechism is a helpful place to start. Time is a great solvent of irrelevance. If a creed or confession or catechism has been in existence and proved useful for centuries, then one can be reasonably confident that it does not contain a lot of irrelevant or peripheral fluff but rather things that are of perennial importance to Christians.

In my own tradition, that of Presbyterianism, the Westminster Confession and the Larger and Shorter Catechisms were composed in the 1640s as sweeping statements of the essentials of the Christian faith. They have in the years since been subject to some revisions. For example, the American version has been revised to eliminate the positive link between state and church, known as the Establishment Principle, in order to bring the documents into line with the American view of the matter. But the vast majority of the text of the Westminster Standards remains unchanged. Any church using them as a guide to the whole counsel of God will find a very helpful resource for seeing what is of key importance.

Some might respond and say that such historic documents are of limited usefulness today, when wider society presses matters such as gay marriage or transgenderism upon us. There is truth in this: the Westminster Confession does not address such issues directly in the way that pastors might have to do so, but it does contain positive teaching about what it means to be human and what are the nature and purposes of marriage. These provide solid, general conceptual foundations by which the church can approach contemporary challenges, and they do so in a way that sets the immediate problems of our day in the context of the broader framework of perennial Christian truth. In short, such confessions help us not only to see that certain things are wrong but to see why they are so in terms of God's truth as a whole. A pedagogical strategy based on these as guides would seem to be a highly desirable part of any church's life in our present circumstances.

Shape Intuitions through Biblical Worship

Expressive individualism in the form in which we find it in contemporary society is problematic for the ways in which it places individuals and their own desires—we might even say their own egos—at the center of the moral universe. Yet we must be careful not to miss the important truths it contains, such as its underlying commitment to the notion of universal human dignity, regardless of where we are placed in the earthly hierarchy. Furthermore, its emphasis upon our inner psychological space and upon our emotions and our desires is not in itself wrong. It is wrong only when it makes such things effectively ends in themselves. God has created us as beings with emotions and desires. We are intentional creatures, not simply animals of instinct, and our inner thought processes are vital to who we are. And that means that we need to acknowledge that inner psychological space and shape its intuitions in the right way.

Augustine's autobiography, *Confessions*, is one of the classics of Christian literature. The book is preoccupied with his inner life as Augustine recalls key incidents from his earlier life. What is interesting, however, is that Augustine's inward move of reflection does not terminate there but always ends up moving outward toward God. Ultimately, his feelings are set in the context of, and corrected by, the larger truth that is God and his revelation in Christ. We might say a similar dynamic applies in the Psalms. The various psalmists speak with honesty, often brutal and painful, about their feelings toward friends, enemies, and even God himself. But this is never for the purpose of self-validation or, worse still, a wallowing in self-indulgent self-pity. Rather, it is for the purpose of setting the experiences and the feelings recounted within the context of God's great truths.

For the church to grasp this truth and shape our psychological intuitions in the biblical way, she needs to think long and hard about one of the central and formative acts of worship: singing. It is no coincidence that the Psalter is a book of corporate praise. Singing such poetry as a community shaped the social imaginary of the Jews. And the church needs to do the same today. Yes, we have been complicit in expressive individualism; no, we do not want to go down the road that leads from Rousseau to Oprah Winfrey and make sentiments the foundation for how we live our lives. But that does not mean that we should therefore eliminate the place of sentiment and emotion in our church lives. Far from it. We need to reform our corporate church lives in a way that forms our inner lives appropriately. And that means choosing worship songs that do not indulge in emotion for the sake of emotion or press upon me that my needs and my desires are the reason God exists. No, we need songs that allow us to understand and express our feelings honestly, but in a way that always leads outward to God and to his truth. And while I do not think, as some do, that the church should sing only psalms, I am inclined to say that singing more psalms—or any psalms if you do not sing them already—would be an excellent place to start.

Think about it: the Psalms present a view of the Christian life that is marked by joy but that also knows sorrow and loss. They set the struggles of the present in the context of God's great actions in times past and promises for the future. They help us to understand our status as strangers in a strange land. By setting forth a grand picture of God and the promise of future rest, they help us to keep perspective—theological and emotional—on the events of the present, whether personal, such as illness, or social, such as the disturbing transformations outlined in this book. We are creatures of emotions and sentiments, and we are fallen. Therefore, we need songs of redemption to help restore them to their proper context.

Natural Law and the Theology of the Body

The church also needs to recover natural law and a theology of the body. Roman Catholics have a long tradition with regard to the former and, in the person of Pope John Paul II, a brilliant teacher of the latter. While Protestantism at the time of the Reformation had a rich appreciation for natural law, it is something that has died away in the last two centuries.

So what is natural law? Put simply, it is the idea that the world in which we live is not simply morally indifferent "stuff" but possesses in itself a moral structure. Our bodies in particular have a profound significance. We connect to others through our bodies. We are dependent on others because of our bodies. Our bodies are not containers that we happen to inhabit and animate. They are in a deep and significant way integral to our identity, to ourselves. Bodies have strengths and weaknesses, some specific to the individual for sure, but many shared by us all. This means that human beings—human bodies—are made to flourish in some ways and not in others.

All of us understand this in what we might call a technical, morally neutral way. I cannot climb up the Empire State Building and jump off the top expecting to flourish. I am not made to fly under my own strength. My bodily constitution places restrictions on what I can and cannot do. Natural law is the extension of this idea into the realm of morals. Thus, for example, the dependency of a newborn child upon her mother is natural, as is the obligation of the mother to protect and nurture the child to the best of her ability. It would, therefore, be immoral for the mother to abandon the child in the woods, to be eaten by wild animals. Or if we assume that life is a natural good, then the termination of that life by another is wrong, a move against nature, and therefore murder is wrong.

When it comes to the central concerns of this book—sex and identity—the idea of natural law is of obvious help. Without wishing to be too explicit, male and female bodies are made to fit together sexually in certain ways and not in others. Men's bodies are simply not made to fit sexually with other men's bodies. Almost everyone is born with a body that types them at birth as male or female, and for good reason: those bodies have different capacities and perform certain different functions. In each case, we can say that nature—or the natural law—points to the boundaries of what is and is not behavior that will lead to human beings flourishing.

One response to this might be that human sin means that such arguments will have no force with the wider world. Does gay sex raise the risk of AIDS or cancer? Well, the world will respond by putting money into relevant medical research and seek to develop drugs and treatments that eliminate or mitigate the problem. Do some people think they were born in the wrong bodies? Surgery and hormones can be applied to make the psychological conviction a physical reality. In each case, the assumption is that nature is just "stuff," something to be overcome as and when it obstructs us from doing or being whatever we want.

This objection has weight. Yes, the world is in rebellion against God and in thrall to the idea that we can be anything we wish; thus, every appeal to any kind of external authority is likely to be met with derision or denial. But that is not why I am recommending reflection on natural law and the theology of the body. These are not so much apologetic tools for addressing the world (though they may have more usefulness there than many will admit); they are important parts of a persuasive pedagogical strategy within the church herself.

Take, for example, a young Christian wrestling with whether homosexuality is right or wrong. A pastor might point such a person to certain biblical texts that indicate it is wrong because it contradicts God's will with regard to the purpose of sex. That may well be enough to convince the young Christian, but I suspect that he might still wrestle with a further question: Does God forbid homosexuality simply because he is a mean tyrant? Is it just that he does not want my gay friends to be happy? Why has he prohibited such behavior?

Older Christians can no longer assume that biblical ethics make sense to younger Christians because the social imaginary in which they operate is so different to the one many of us grew up in. And that means we need to work harder at explaining not simply the content but also the rationale of Christian morality. Now, in this scenario above, it is therefore helpful not simply to point to what the Bible teaches in a few texts but also to show that those texts make sense within the larger picture. And this larger picture has both a broad biblical side, where sex is a function of what the Bible teaches about human personhood, and also a "natural law" side, where, for example, the sexual complementarity of male and female bodies is relevant, as is the evidence of damage done to the physical body by certain sexual practices. It is not that nature here offers the decisive argument; yet it does help to show that biblical teaching is not an arbitrary imposition on nature but instead correlates with it. In other words, it assists us in showing that God's commands make sense, given the way the world actually is.

Neither Despair nor Optimism

Finally, the church needs to respond to this present age by avoiding the temptations of despair and optimism. To fall into the former would be to fail to take seriously the promise that the church will win in the end because the gates of hell shall not prevail against her. To engage in the latter is simply to prepare the stage for deeper despair later. And both will feed inaction, one out of a sense of impotence, the other out of naivete.

There is an alternative. Last year in conversation with my friend the journalist and Orthodox Christian Rod Dreher, I commented on the bleak outlook of much of his writing and alluded to him as pessimistic. He laughingly rejected the adjective. "I am neither pessimistic nor optimistic," he said, "but I am hopeful." And hope, of course, is not optimism. Pollyanna was an optimist, as was Mr. Micawber. Optimism is the belief that everything will be fine if everyone just sits tight and waits.

Christian hope, however, is realistic. It understands that this world is a vale of tears, that things here are not as they should be, and that, in the words of Gerard Manley Hopkins, all life death does end. This world is not the Christian's home, and so we should not expect it to provide us with home comforts. That is not to say we should not be grateful for the good things we do have here and now. I thank God that I still live in a country with greater freedoms than, say, China. I thank God that I live in a time and a place where I have access to good healthcare, that I have a job I enjoy, and that I have a loving family. I pray that such things will continue for me and also be the same for others. But I am also aware that the world is fallen, that the gospel does not promise me necessarily the life of ease and comfort I currently have, and that my calling, as that of all Christians, is to live faithfully in the time and place I have been set. And that means that when things in this world go awry, or when I am faced with changes that bring suffering to me or to my loved ones or to society at large, I must not despair, I must work to the best of my ability to right such wrongs, and I must also remember that the real meaning of my life and that of others is not found in the here and now but in the hereafter. Suffering here and now may at times be terrible, even unbearable, but it is never meaningless. No, it finds its meaning in the life, death, resurrection, ascension, and return of the Lord Jesus Christ.

And so this book comes to an end. The world in which we live seems set to be entering a new, chaotic, uncharted and dark era. But we should not despair. We need to prepare ourselves, be informed, know what we believe and why we believe it, worship God in a manner that forms us as true disciples and pilgrims, intellectually and intuitively, and keep before our eyes the unbreakable promises that the Lord has made and confirmed in Jesus Christ. This is not a time for hopeless despair nor naïve optimism. Yes, let us lament the ravages of the fall as they play out in the distinctive ways that our generation has chosen. But let that lamentation be the context for sharpening our identity as the people of God and our hunger for the great consummation that awaits at the marriage feast of the Lamb.

Study Questions

1. How have you become complicit in today's expressive individualistic culture?

2. In what ways have you become a consumer of churches?

3. What do you think are the benefits and challenges of having so many denominations within the Protestant church?

4. How has this book changed how you view specific hot topics in today's culture?

5. How has this book equipped you to renew and defend your biblical convictions?

Glossary

AIDS crisis. The 1980s outbreak of HIV in the United States.

Brandenburg v. Ohio. The 1969 Supreme Court case in which the court replaced the Clear and Present Danger Test with the Imminent Lawless Action Test, enforcing protection of free speech.

cancel culture. The term applied to a culture where advocates of viewpoints regarded as obnoxious by dominant social groups are silenced by preventing them from having platforms to speak or write. A culture where censorship of unpopular opinions has come to be regarded as a social virtue.

dualism. The division of concepts into separate ideas.

expressive individualism. The belief that each person must act based on expressing his or her core feelings and intuition.

Feuerbach, Ludwig. The German philosopher (1804–1872) and student of Hegel whose writings about the futility of religion influenced Karl Marx.

gender dysphoria. The psychological condition where someone does not identify with the biological sex of their body.

Goethe, Johann Wolfgang von. A German writer (1749–1832) with secularized views of sexuality and religion.

Gorsuch, Justice Neil. The Supreme Court justice (b. 1967) nominated by President Donald Trump in 2017.

Hegel, G. W. F. A German philosopher (1770–1831) whose work emphasized rationality as the only basis for reality.

intersex. A biological condition where a person has the sex characteristics of both male and female.

Jenner, Caitlyn (Bruce). A former Olympic gold medal decathlete (b. 1949) who was born biologically male and has since transitioned to live life as a transgender female.

Kant, Immanuel. A German philosopher and Enlightenment thinker (1724–1804) whose work emphasized rationality in morality.

#MeToo. The pop cultural movement in twenty-first-century America to bring awareness of sexual harassment and abuse and encourage victims to make allegations.

normative authority. Creating a norm or standard.

Oedipus complex. The Freudian theory that young children sexually desire the parent of the opposite sex.

original sin. The belief that humans innately have a tendency to sin due to the fall of Adam and Eve, written about by Saint Augustine (354–430).

Pentecost. The event when the Holy Spirit descended onto earth.

Playboy **(Hugh Hefner, 1926–2017).** A men's lifestyle magazine, beginning in 1953, notorious for publishing semi-pornographic material.

Pollyanna and Mr. Micawber. Characters representing optimism and hopefulness, respectively belonging to the books *Pollyanna* by Eleanor H. Porter and *David Copperfield* by Charles Dickens.

Prepolitical. A term used to describe relationships and organizations that exist for the common pursuit of life but which do not involve the typical political conflicts of the public square.

Reformation. Sixteenth-century reform within the Catholic Church that led to the institutional fragmentation of the church.

Religious Affections. A 1746 book by preacher and theologian Jonathan Edwards (1703–1758) regarding the process of conversion and its psychological impact.

Romanticism. Movement in arts and literature in the late-eighteenth and early-ninetenth centuries embracing the primacy of the individual and focusing on the force of nature and the natural world.

Schenck v. United States. 1919 Supreme Court case in which the court ruled that the government could restrict free speech if it presented a clear and present danger to national interests.

sexual revolution. The liberalization of attitudes toward sex and sexuality that began in the West in the 1960s.

social imaginary. The set of socially conditioned intuitions by which a person relates to the world in a nonreflective way.

The Picture of Dorian Gray. The controversial novel by Oscar Wilde in which the main character sells his soul in order to maintain his hedonistic lifestyle of youth, beauty, and pleasure.

To the Lighthouse. The 1927 feminist novel by Virginia Woolf centered on women in marriage and society.

transgenderism. The state in which one does not identify with one's biological sex and attempts to transition into the opposite gender.

Trotskyism. A Russian branch of revolutionary Marxism.

Unabomber. Theodore Kaczynski (b. 1942), an American domestic terrorist who murdered three people and was responsible for injuring twenty-three more in his nationwide bombing spree against those whom he believed were advancing industrialization.

Watergate tapes. Recordings of the Richard Nixon (1913–1994) presidency that exposed Nixon's illegal activity.

Wilde, Oscar. The Irish writer (1854–1900) whose work reflected the movements of aestheticism and decadence.

Yogyakarta Principles. The human rights protection rules about sex and gender named after the Indonesian city where the meeting took place at which they were agreed.

Notes

Foreword

1. Michael J. Sandel, "The Procedural Republic and the Unencumbered Self," *Political Theory* 12, no. 1 (February, 1984), 81–96.
2. Robert N. Bellah et al., *Habits of the Heart: Individualism and Commitment in American Life* (Berkeley: University of California Press, 1996).
3. Philip Rieff, *The Triumph of the Therapeutic: Uses of Faith after Freud*, 40th anniversary ed. (1966; repr., Wilmington: ISI Books, 2006).
4. Joe Biden (@JoeBiden), Twitter, January 25, 2020, 12:20 p.m., https://twitter.com/JoeBiden/status/1221135646107955200.

Chapter 1: Welcome to This Strange New World

1. Robert N. Bellah et al., *Habits of the Heart: Individualism and Commitment in American Life* (Berkeley: University of California Press, 1996), 333–34.
2. Charles Taylor, *A Secular Age* (Cambridge, MA: Belknap, 2007), 475.
3. Taylor, *A Secular Age*, 171–72.

Chapter 2: Romantic Roots

1. Jean-Jacques Rousseau, *Confessions*, ed. Patrick Coleman, trans. Angela Scholar (Oxford: Oxford University Press, 2000), 5, 270.
2. Jean-Jacques Rousseau, *The Discourses and Other Early Political Writings*, ed. and trans. Victor Gourevitch, Cambridge Texts in the History of Political Thought (Cambridge: Cambridge University Press, 1997), 7–8.
3. Jean-Jacques Rousseau, *The Social Contract and Other Later Political Writings*, ed. and trans. Victor Gourevitch, Cambridge Texts in the History of Political Thought (Cambridge: Cambridge University Press, 1997), 41.

4. Mary Wollstonecraft, *Letters Written in Sweden, Norway, and Denmark* (Oxford: Oxford University Press, 2009), 39.

5. Samuel Taylor Coleridge, "The Eolian Harp," Poetry Foundation (website), accessed July 2, 2021, https://www.poetryfoundation.org/.

6. William Wordsworth, *The Major Works*, ed. Stephen Gill (Oxford: Oxford University Press, 2000), 622; wording modernized.

Chapter 3: Prometheus Unbound

1. Ludwig Feuerbach, *The Essence of Christianity*, trans. George Eliot (New York: Harper and Row, 1957), 14.

2. Karl Marx and Friedrich Engels, *Marx on Religion*, ed. John Raines (Philadelphia, PA: Temple University Press, 2002), 171.

3. Friedrich Nietzsche, *The Gay Science*, trans. Walter Kaufmann (New York: Vintage, 1974), §108 (167). First published in German in 1887.

4. Nietzsche, *The Gay Science*, §125 (181–82).

5. Modris Eksteins, *The Rites of Spring: The Great War and the Birth of the Modern Age* (New York: Mariner Books, 2000), 34.

6. Friedrich Nietzsche, *Beyond Good and Evil*, trans. Walter Kaufmann (New York: Vintage, 1989) § 201–3 (112–13).

7. Oscar Wilde, *De Profundis* (New York: Knickerbocker Press, 1909), 73.

8. Oscar Wilde, *The Major Works* (Oxford: Oxford University Press, 2008), 48.

9. Oscar Wilde, *The Soul of Man Under Socialism and Selected Critical Prose* (London: Penguin, 2001), 105.

10. Wilde, *The Soul of Man Under Socialism*, 152.

11. Wilde, *The Soul of Man Under Socialism*, 136.

12. Wilde, *The Soul of Man Under Socialism*, 137.

Chapter 4: Sexualizing Psychology, Politicizing Sex

1. Sigmund Freud, *Civilization and Its Discontents*, trans. James Strachey (New York: W. W. Norton, 1989), 25.

2. Freud, *Civilization and Its Discontents*, 56.

3. Sigmund Freud, *Three Essays on the Theory of Sexuality*, trans. and ed. James Strachey (New York: Basic Books, 2000), 17–18.

4. Freud, *Civilization and Its Discontents*, 73.

5. Sigmund Freud, *The Future of an Illusion*, trans. and ed. James Strachey (New York: W. W. Norton, 1961), 47.

6. Wilhelm Reich, *The Mass Psychology of Fascism*, ed. and trans. Mary Higgins and Chester M. Raphael (New York: Farrar, Straus, and Giroux, 1970), 29.

7. Reich, *The Mass Psychology of Fascism*, 30.

8. Reich, *The Mass Psychology of Fascism*, 30.

9. Wilhelm Reich, *The Sexual Revolution: Toward a Self-Regulating Character Structure*, trans. Therese Pol (New York: Farrar, Straus, and Giroux, 1974), 23.

10. Reich, *The Sexual Revolution*, 25.

11. Reich, *The Sexual Revolution*, 24.

12. Reich, *The Sexual Revolution*, xvi.

13. Augusto Del Noce, *The Crisis of Modernity* (Montreal: McGill-Queen's University Press, 2015), 166.

Chapter 5: The Revolt of the Masses

1. Yuval Levin, *A Time to Build: From Family and Community to Congress and the Campus, How Recommitting to Our Institutions Can Revive the American Dream* (New York: Basic Books, 2020), 33–34.

2. Jason Blakely, *We Built Reality: How Social Science Infiltrated Culture, Politics, and Power* (Oxford: Oxford University Press, 2020), xxvi.

Chapter 6: Plastic People, Liquid World

1. Benedict Anderson, *Imagined Communities: Reflections on the Origin and Spread of Nationalism* (London: Verso, 2016).

2. Jean-Paul Sartre, *Existentialism Is a Humanism*, trans. Carol Macomber (New Haven, CT: Yale University Press, 2007), 29.

Chapter 7: The Sexual Revolution of the LGBTQ+

1. Simone de Beauvoir, *The Second Sex*, trans. Constance Borde and Sheila Malovany-Chevallier, with an introduction by Judith Thurman (New York: Vintage, 2011), 283.

2. Boston Women's Health Book Collective, *Our Bodies, Ourselves* (New York: Touchstone, 2011), 85.

3. Janice Raymond, *Transsexual Empire: The Making of the She-Male* (New York: Teachers College Press, 1994), xx.

4. Lucy Clarke-Billings, "Germaine Greer in Transgender Rant: 'Just Because You Lop Off Your Penis . . . It Doesn't Make You a Woman,'" *Telegraph*, October 26, 2015, https://www.telegraph.co.uk/.

5. Germaine Greer, *The Whole Woman* (New York: Random House, 1999), 80.

6. *The Yogyakarta Principles: Principles on the Application of International Human Rights Law in Relation to Sexual Orientation and Gender Identity* (2007), 8, accessed July 6, 2021, https://yogyakarta principles.org/.

7. *Yogyakarta Principles*, 8.

8. *Yogyakarta Principles*, 11.

9. *Yogyakarta Principles*, 27.
10. Bostock v. Clayton County, 590 U.S. ___ (2020), https://www.supreme court.gov/opinions/19pdf/17-1618_hfci.pdf.
11. Text available at "Preventing and Combating Discrimination on the Basis of Gender Identity or Sexual Orientation," January 20, 2021, https://www.whitehouse.gov/briefing-room/presidential-actions/2021/01/20/executive-order-preventing-and-combating-discrimination-on-basis-of-gender-identity-or-sexual-orientation/.

Chapter 8: Life, Liberty, and the Pursuit of Happiness

1. United States v. Windsor, 699 F. 3d 169 (2013), https://www.law.cornell.edu/supremecourt/text/12-307.
2. Planned Parenthood of Southeastern Pennsylvania v. Casey, 505 U.S. 833, 851 (1992), https://www.law.cornell.edu/supremecourt/text/505/833.
3. For the full text of the decision, see Schenck v. United States, 249 U.S. 47 (1919), https://www.law.cornell.edu/supremecourt/text/249/47%26 quot%3B.
4. For the full text of the decision, see Brandenburg v. Ohio, 395 U.S. 444 (1969), https://www.law.cornell.edu/supremecourt/text/395/444.
5. "Repressive Tolerance" was reprinted, with an afterword reflecting on the student unrest of 1968, in Robert Paul Wolff, Barrington Moore Jr., and Herbert Marcuse, *A Critique of Pure Tolerance* (Boston, MA: Beacon, 1970), 81–123.
6. Marcuse, "Repressive Tolerance," 111.
7. "Mission," *Beyond the Green: Collective of Middlebury Voices* (blog), accessed July 6, 2021, https://beyondthegreenmidd.wordpress.com/.

Chapter 9: Strangers in This Strange New World

1. Philip Rieff, *The Triumph of the Therapeutic: Uses of Faith after Freud* (1966; repr., Wilmington, DE: ISI Books, 2006), 30.
2. For an accessible translation, see St. Augustine, *City of God*, trans. Henry Bettenson (New York: Penguin, 2004).

Index

Also Available from Carl R. Trueman

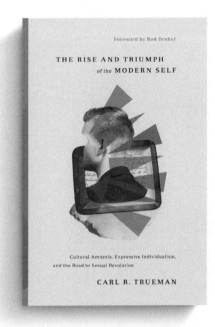

The Rise and Triumph of the Modern Self offers a more extensive presentation and application of the topics covered in *Strange New World*.

Carl Trueman analyzes the development of the sexual revolution as a symptom—rather than the cause—of the human search for identity. He surveys the past, brings clarity to the present, and gives guidance for the future as Christians navigate the culture in humanity's ever-changing quest for identity.

For more information, visit **crossway.org**.

Go Deeper with the Study Guide and Video Study

The **Strange New World Study Guide** walks through each of the book's 9 chapters, summarizing key points, posing thought-provoking questions, and providing Bible verses for further reading.

Each 10–12 minute session of the **Strange New World Video Study** is taught by Carl Trueman and covers one chapter from the book. The video study can be used in conjunction with the book, the *Strange New World Study Guide*, or both.

For more information, visit **crossway.org**.